Freedom
from the
Performance
Trap

Other Victor Books by David Seamands

Healing for Damaged Emotions
Healing for Damaged Emotions Workbook
Healing of Memories
Putting Away Childish Things
Putting Away Childish Things Workbook

Freedom from the Performance Trap

David A. Seamands

formerly titled *Healing Grace*

VICTOR BOOKS®
A DIVISION OF SCRIPTURE PRESS PUBLICATIONS INC.
USA CANADA ENGLAND

Recommended Dewey Decimal Classification: 234.1
Suggested Subject Heading: RECOVERY

ISBN: 0-89693-986-3

6   7   8   9   10   11   12   13   Printing/Year   95   94

Contents.

One.   THE MIRACLE OF GRACE
9

Two.   BARRIERS TO GRACE
25

Three.   PARENTAL GRACE—OR DYSGRACE
39

Four.   HOW IT ALL BEGAN
55

Five.   THE BAD NEWS
71

Six.   THE CONSEQUENCES OF DYSGRACE
87

Seven.   THE GOOD NEWS
107

Eight.   GRACE AND GUILT
125

Nine.   GRACE AND EMOTIONS
139

Ten.   GRACE AND SELF-ESTEEM
151

Eleven.   GRACE AND NEGATIVE FEELINGS
167

Twelve.   THE PANORAMA OF GOD'S GRACE
185

NOTES
202

To my most influential mentors
Dr. Edwin Lewis of Drew
who got me excited about the theology of grace
and
Dr. E. Stanley Jones of India
who got me excited about the Lord of grace

Preface.

Early in my ministry I discovered that the experience of grace is the most therapeutic factor in emotional and spiritual healing. A doctor who works in a mental hospital in Tennessee put it this way, "Half of my patients could go home in a week if they knew they were forgiven."

The main task in counseling and inner healing is to remove the barriers to forgiveness so that people can receive grace—the gift of God's love freely offered to the undeserving and the unworthy.

Next to God's Word, prayer, and the sacrament of the Lord's Supper, the great hymns of the church rank high in healing efficacy. I have begun each chapter in this book with words from one of Charles Wesley's hymns, filled as they are with both the theology and the wonder of grace. It is fitting that on Wesley's statue in Bristol, England are inscribed the opening words of his hymn, "O Let Me Commend My Saviour to You."

My prayer is that these hymns, so precious to me in my own heritage, will bring healing grace to you.

David A. Seamands
Asbury Theological Seminary
Wilmore, Kentucky
1988

One.

THE MIRACLE
OF GRACE

O for a thousand tongues to sing
My great Redeemer's praise,
The glories of my God and King,
The triumphs of His grace!

Look unto Him, ye nations, own
Your God, ye fallen race;
Look and be saved through faith alone,
Be justified by grace.

As I sat listening to Devadas, a handsome young Indian graduate student, a story I had heard from an old-time camp meeting evangelist flashed across my mind. It was about a skeptic who told a pastor in his local community, "Your Christians seem to have just enough religion to keep them from sinning, but not enough to make them happy. They remind me of a man with a headache. It hurts him to keep it, but he doesn't want to cut off his head."

At the time I was in India serving as the pastor of a downtown, English-speaking church. My family and I had just come from almost ten years of evangelistic work in the villages where our main task had been planting new congregations and church-building among rural, uneducated people. Now we were faced with highly educated city dwellers who were plagued with the usual problems of urban and industrial life.

At the time I didn't recognize the nature of the problem being presented to me. After all, Devadas was one of the finest young adults in our congregation. A deeply committed, Spirit-filled believer from a long-standing Christian family, he lived up to his name, "servant of God." Loyal in attending every service of the church, though it meant a tiring bicycle ride of several miles, he was a thorough student of the Scriptures and a faithful witness among his jeering Hindu colleagues. If necessary, Devadas would have died *for* his Christianity—no question about that. The real question just now was why he seemed to be almost dying *from* it.

That afternoon in 1957, I hadn't the faintest idea that he was describing many of the usual characteristics of Christians caught in the meshes of the performance trap. The only thing both of us knew was that it kept him in emotional and spiritual turmoil.

For well over an hour, he shared his problems with me—his never-ending battle with *the tyranny of the oughts;*

his overhanging sense of *guilt and condemnation;* a high
level of *anxiety;* a sense of *low self-esteem* from constant
self-belittling; denial and repression of negative emotions
such as *anger or depression;* and a *legalism and scrupulosity*
resulting from a damaged, oversensitive conscience.[1]

In my naiveté, it seemed obvious to me that Devadas
just wasn't as *spiritual* as he ought to be. After all, I was
only a decade out of seminary and filled with answers for
most *every* problem. So I began to counsel him the only
way I knew. Like many pastors I thought counseling was a
one-to-one preaching session with a captive audience.

However, to all of my sincere questions with their implied and well-meaning suggestions, he kept giving me
answers that just didn't fit my simplistic solutions.

"Brother Devadas, have you been reading your
Bible regularly? If you'd increase your time spent in
the Word, you would find greater peace and victory.
I'm sure this would restore the joy of your salvation."

"But Pastor Seamands, I've already done that. In
fact, for some time now, I've been reading an extra
chapter from both the Old and New Testaments
every day."

"I see. . . . Well, how is your prayer life? You
remember in a recent sermon I quoted one of the
great saints who said, 'Prayer is not simply the *prepa-
ration for* the battle, prayer *is* the battle.' " (I had
been impressed with that and was hoping everyone
else had been too.)

"Yes, Pastor. I wrote it in the margin of my Bible
that morning and I have increased my prayer time.
But to be perfectly honest with you, neither of these
have helped much. In fact, as strange as it may
sound, I seem to be somewhat worse. Something inside keeps telling me I *ought* to read even more, and I
should pray even more. I cannot understand it, but

*I never seem to be able to do quite enough. In fact, that's
what seems to be the whole problem.''*

I was stumped. I believed he was telling me the truth. I
knew better than to ask him about fellowship with other
Christians or witnessing—I had seen his record in those
areas. Somewhere in the midst of my frustration, the Holy
Spirit strongly suggested, "Why don't you just shut up and
listen carefully to what he is saying? You've been so anxious to impress him with your answers that you haven't
really heard his questions."

For the first time having ears to listen, I actually *heard*
the meaning of what he was saying. More important still,
I began to *feel* his pain. *"I feel like I ought to do more. I
should do more, I could do more. And I honestly try, but I
never seem to do enough."*

I later realized I had been ambushed by something quite
different from the spiritual malaise that results from ne-
glecting the regular means of grace and growth.

This unforgettable experience took place over thirty
years ago. From that hand-to-hand, eyeball-to-eyeball,
heart-to-heart encounter, there emerged the hazy begin-
nings of what in the years following would become a ministry to many hurting and disheartened Christians. These
sensitive, sincere, highly motivated, and extremely hard-
working people were trapped on the treadmill of spiritual
performance, with no way to get off. In a sense, they were
captives in a prison which was at least partially of their
own making.

Performance

Devadas had said it all in his summary description. "I
ought to, I should, I could, I try, but I never seem to be
able to do enough." That's the inescapable bondage, the
vicious circle from which there is no escape through bigger

and better performance. That's the Avis button core of the curse, the horrible hub from which all the spokes emanate to hold the wheel of the treadmill in place.

While there are varying degrees of performance concentration, the syndrome itself is a kind of disease, a malignant virus at the heart of every human being. It is the ultimate lie behind myriads of ordinary lies, persuading us that every relationship in life is based on performance, that is, on what we do.

This lie insists that *everything* depends on how well we perform—

our salvation and status—our relationship with God

our sense of self-worth—our relationship with ourselves

our sense of security and belongingness—our relationship with others

our sense of achievement and success—our relationship with society around us.

Just as there are different degrees of any disease, so there are different levels of intensity in performance orientation. They vary from mild to strong, from severe to critical, from the fairly normal to the abnormal and even pathological. Performance-oriented Christians represent a wide range of despairing humanity. There are the very young in the Christian life, who are struggling to believe in a grace which just seems too good to be true. There are those who, like the Galatians, started out living by grace but now are mixing law (performance) and grace (gift). There are the perfectionists who feel sure nothing they do is ever good enough for God, others, or themselves.

Also represented are some deeply troubled persons with abnormal and even pathological symptoms, some of whom constantly battle against compulsions, like hand-washing; or obsessions, like a persuasion that they have committed the unpardonable sin; or phobias, like fear of contamination from germs. These disturbed individuals may receive some help from a Christian counselor or a book like this, but they usually require the help of psychiatrists and even special medication. In this book, I am addressing Christians who experience a more normal range of performance orientation and perfectionism. They do not display some of the extremes we have described, but they are hurting people, spiritually bound up, emotionally hung up, and relationally tied up.

I am convinced that the basic cause of some of the most disturbing emotional/spiritual problems which trouble evangelical Christians is the failure to receive and live out God's unconditional grace, and the corresponding failure to offer that grace to others. I encounter this problem in the counseling room more than any other single hangup. Dr. David Stoop, a Christian clinical psychologist in California, confirms my findings as he says, "It wasn't that I was looking for perfectionism to be a problem. It just seemed to keep cropping up as an issue with almost everyone who came to see me for counseling.[2] Unfortunately, he too counsels mostly Christians.

Pain

Before I describe some of the major problems which plague performance-bound Christians, I would like you to get the *feel* of the matter. Let me quote some statements which have come to me in letters from readers or notes from counselees. They are all cries for help and reveal some of the most painful symptoms of the disease. In these word pictures, you may identify yourself, or someone you live with. Please note the italicized phrases, since we will look at them shortly.

I have been a struggling Christian for the past thirteen years. My problem is that *I am never at peace* and am always trying to be good—that is, *to be better. I am so afraid of making mistakes.*

14

I am a college student and a believer in Christ. Your article really hit home to me. *I am always feeling that kind of anxiety, guilt, and condemnation.* These feelings invade my day-to-day thought processes. I cannot perform a task, read a book, or practice my music without *feeling I am being judged.* Several years ago I accepted Christ as my Saviour, but I feel *everything I do is not good enough for my Lord.*

It's difficult for me to attend church anymore, because our minister stresses regular Bible reading. I want to read God's Word; but *whenever I read the Bible, I feel the Lord is "putting the whammy on me"* for what I am doing and where I am going with my life.

That particular chapter was a picture of me exactly! Even my husband said it fit me to a tee. I have all kinds of *unrealistic expectations.* Also, *I attempt impossible performances* and try to get God's approval by keeping a lot of legalistic rules. *I thought I had to earn His love, and that caused me to almost take my life.*

I want to be used more effectively for the Lord, but *feel so unworthy and useless. I am such a failure I can't stand to live with myself.* I had such a wonderful conversion and in many ways am a "new creature in Christ." I really identified with your descriptions of *anger and resentment. It's almost like I go through a hate cycle against the people I love the most. Afterward I am so sorry and get very depressed.* I guess I'm *angriest* because I'm not having spiritual victory.

I am a missionary. God has used me to win souls. *I know all the answers,* all the Scriptures, and can quote the exact chapter and verse. But it is *all in my head. The God I serve is never pleased with me* and is certainly nothing like the gracious loving God I say I believe in—and tell others about. *Why can't I practice what I preach? I feel like a fake.*

I've come a long ways in counseling and God has made many changes in me. *I know I have to let go of the phony "spiritual" person I've tried to be for so many years. But I'm scared to death because I don't know who I really am and what I may turn out to be. Is it possible to be terrified and excited at the same time?*

I try hard to be loving, but I'm so critical and judgmental, so hard on my spouse and kids. The slightest failure on their part and I get angry and explode. Then I *feel guilty and get depressed.* My family is so loving and forgiving—but that only makes matters worse. It's almost like *a pattern that keeps repeating itself.*

It seems the harder I try, the harder I fall. When *I get exhausted and quit trying at all,* I really do feel condemned. It seems like *a pattern* of some kind.

The italicized words and sentences clearly describe the major areas of defeat and despair in the lives of Christians who have not yet fully grasped what it is to live a grace-based life. They also pinpoint the damage and pain which need to be healed before these people can enjoy a grace-full life.

• Continuous feelings of guilt, condemnation, and the judgment and disapproval of God. Again and again Christians tell me, "I feel guilty almost all the time." When I ask, "Aren't there times when you don't feel guilty, or when you have a sense of being at peace with God?" they often answer, "Not really, because then *I feel guilty for not feeling guilty!*"

Such guilt is not related to specific sinful acts or attitudes. Instead, it is a general, global sense of guilt which
penetrates the entire personality somewhat as an early
morning fog fills a valley. And like a fog, it varies in
intensity. Some Christians live in a mild haze of divine
disapproval which always surrounds them. And since
they've never known anything different, they wrongly presume all Christians live that way. With others, the fog is
so thick they are almost immobilized. They can hardly
move in any direction or make even small decisions. They
know they'll feel guilty in any case—it's "damned if you
do and damned if you don't." It would be difficult to
exaggerate the emotional pain and spiritual despair of such
Christians.

• A sense of worthlessness, with feelings of low self-
esteem and recurring inward assaults of self-belittling and
even self-despising. There is so much misunderstanding
regarding the term *self-esteem* it is best to clarify what we
mean. The ordinary dictionary definition of *esteem* is "to
value highly, have regard for; to prize or respect." When
we speak of self-esteem, we mean that individuals place
value on themselves as persons and consider themselves as
having worth. Performance-grounded Christians do *not*
feel good about themselves as persons, in spite of what
they may have accomplished. However successful they
may be in the eyes of others, they invariably belittle themselves—they literally tell themselves to "be little" so that
they will not forget the small value they put on themselves, and their imagined insignificance in the sight of
God and other people.

• A sense of phoniness and unreality, a feeling of being
an empty fake, of having somehow lost touch with their
real selves and not knowing who they really are. Because
of the many contradictions such Christians find in their
lives, they feel a loss of their own unique selfhood. There
is such a chasm between *who they are* and *who they ought to*

be, meaning, *who they ought to be because they are Christians,* that the pain is unbearable. They become so alienated from the self they deeply dislike that they try to deny its existence. But it keeps asserting itself to remind them of its presence. This comes out in statements such as, "I know all the answers, but they're only in my head. I don't really feel them in my heart. I tell others of Christ, but at a gut level I don't feel or live the Christian life. I'm scared to find out who I am, and terrified to let others know what I'm really like." Of course, such self-contradiction drains both their desire and their power to effectively witness for Christ. Or if they do so out of a dogged determination to do their duty, they simply feel a greater sense of hypocrisy and emptiness. The saddest thing about these people is the loss of the real person, that true and unique selfhood God has given to them and planned to use for His purposes.

● Many negative emotions, especially anxiety and anger, which result in irrational fears, smoldering resentments, outbursts of rage, excessive mood swings and depression. If being accepted and loved depended on how well we performed, it's not hard to see why rage would be the inevitable consequence. We would be in a state of constant anxiety, and any failure would lead to anger at ourselves and others. This vicious circle of anger and resentment unfortunately includes anger at God, because He doesn't seem to be coming through with His promises.

These ungraced people, having little grace to give, become ungracious toward others. They have the same performance standards for other people as they do for themselves. They feel as resentful and angry against the failures of others as they do against their own shortcomings. When the pressure gets too great, they may slide into the depression which comes from frozen rage, the slow burn of resentments, and an inevitable blowup. All this leads to our final symptom.

• Difficulties with interpersonal relationships, especially where intimacy is involved. In the more shallow contacts of life, most performance-oriented people can function fairly well. Many of them are hardworking, quiet, controlled, and sometimes seem to be the "gentle Jesus, meek and mild" type. But when emotional distance lessens, when a relationship deepens and some degree of closeness is required, then many of the factors we have been describing can emerge and become disruptive, deeply affecting their ability to make and keep friends.

But it is within marriage and parenthood we see the greatest devastation. Let's face it, performance-oriented Christians are hard to live with. They are hard on themselves, hard on their spouses, and hard on their kids. Much of my marriage and family counseling involves partners of this kind. Someone has said, "Perfectionists are those who take great pains and give them to others." To which I would add, "Mostly in the neck!" It was the great Sam Shoemaker who stated, "Everyone *has* a problem, *is* a problem, or *has to live with* a problem." We could restate this, "Perfectionists have a problem, are a problem, and create a problem for those who live with them."

These are the five major symptoms of performance-orientation which need healing grace. However, there is one more important factor that must be part of this introductory chapter.

Pervasive Personality Pattern
The final two letters I quoted from, earlier in this chapter, both contain the word *pattern*. The dictionary tells us a pattern is "a design of natural or accidental origin; a composite of traits or features characteristic of an individual."[3] It is very essential we understand that the Christian who lives a performance-based life does not have an isolated problem in some hidden cupboard of his life that pops out

once in a while to cause occasional emotional and spiritual upheavals. Rather, this pattern is a lifestyle, an all-inclusive *way of being*, a faulty manner of perceiving, thinking, feeling, willing, acting, reacting, and relating. This wrong way of *being* results in a wrong way of *doing*; that is, *a wrong way of coping with life and relating to people.*

The opposite of performance-orientation—a grace-based, grace-oriented life—is also a pattern of being. Such a way of life is more than a basic experience of Christ, such as conversion and the new birth, or being filled with the Spirit, or experiencing occasional times of spiritual highs. A lifestyle which becomes God's right way of *being* is lived out as the right way of *doing*—coping with life's situations and relationships. It's important that we see both the problem and the solution in this same light—as all-pervasive *wrong* and *right* ways of living life and relating to people.

This is why at the very start we must make clear there are no quick cures, no speedy solutions. Neither a miraculous Christian experience nor an instantaneous inner healing is likely to free one from the bonds of the performance trap, especially in its extreme perfectionistic forms. No one believes more than I do in the necessity of the new birth and life in the Spirit as *the* basic ingredients of the Christian life. However, I also believe that many Christians with damaged emotions and unhealed memories need a special kind of inner healing to enable them to live truly victorious lives. All this I find to be in complete agreement with biblical principles, but I consistently warn against solutions that are more magic than miracle, and sow confusion in the hearts of hurting Christians. I spend a disproportionate amount of counseling time trying to pick up the pieces of disillusioned Christians who have unsuccessfully tried some instant cure.

I want to remind you that this warning includes the book you are now reading. Gaining a better understanding of the nature of your problem will not free you from the unhealthy and frustrating performance treadmill. As important as insight and knowledge are, they do not automatically heal or change. The notion that they do is an ancient Greek fallacy, further developed by Freud and, unfortunately, continued even by some present-day Christian psychologists. Paul unmasks this error in his crystal-clear statement, "I do not understand what I do. For what I want to do, I do not do. . . . For I have the desire to do what is good, but I cannot carry it out" (Romans 7:15, 18). Awareness and insight are of tremendous help in many ways, especially in showing us *what* we need to look for and *how* we need to pray. They also reveal those areas of our lives where we need *healing grace in order to fully live out the saving and sanctifying grace we have experienced in Christ.* While healing grace *may* at times include points of *crisis,* it will *always* be a *process* of changing our patterns of life.

From Servant to Son
This is what happened to Devadas, the young man I introduced to you at the beginning. As we began meeting together for regular counseling and prayer, we discovered several areas where there was a real deficiency of grace. Christians in India are a small minority of the total population; understandably, they sometimes feel the need to prove themselves before their non-Christian neighbors. For Devadas, this had resulted in a legalistic and joyless home life where acceptance and approval were highly conditional.

Do you remember the picture of the Elder Brother in Luke 15, who was angry when his brother came home and was met by the father's grace and a feast of celebration? "He answered his father, 'Look! All these years I've been slaving for you and never disobeyed your orders. Yet you never gave me even a young goat so I could celebrate with my friends' " (Luke 15:29). It was in this story that Devadas discovered himself, as the Holy Spirit slowly peeled away his meticulous striving and showed him a graceless and critical heart.

One Sunday I referred to John Wesley as an example in a sermon. Wesley, son of the parsonage, member of Oxford's Holy Club, an ordained Anglican clergyman and foreign missionary, was a devout seeker after personal holiness. But despite all his sacrificial service and good works, he did not find peace with God, and called himself "an almost Christian." Then on May 24, 1738 he discovered grace, while listening to someone read Luther's Preface to the Book of Romans. In Wesley's now well-known words,

> About a quarter before nine, while he was describing the change which God works in the heart through faith in Christ, I felt my heart strangely warmed. I felt I did trust in Christ, Christ alone, for salvation; and an assurance was given me, that He had taken away my sins, even mine, and saved me from the law of sin and death.

Wesley said that he became "an altogether Christian," and that whereas before he had the religion of a "servant," now he had that of a "son."

When Devadas came next to see me, he was visibly excited. "Until Sunday I never realized that I have been *literally* living up to my name—'servant of God.' I have been thinking and feeling and living not like a family member should, but like a servant does." Since everyone in India clearly understands the difference between the two, I said to him, "Devadas, let's do some role playing. You be the servant in the family and I'll be the son. Let's live out a day in their lives, from morning to bedtime, and see what the differences are." He agreed. Before long we were really into it, putting into words the wide differences between our roles.

The servant is accepted and appreciated on the basis of *what he does*, the child on the basis of *who he is*.

The servant starts the day *anxious and worried*, wondering if his work will really please his master. The child *rests in the secure love* of his family.

The servant is accepted because of his *workmanship*, the son or daughter because of a *relationship*.

The servant is accepted because of his *productivity and performance*. The child belongs because of his *position as a person*.

At the end of the day, the servant has peace of mind only if he is sure he has *proven his worth by his work. The next morning his anxiety begins again.* The child can be *secure all day, and know that tomorrow won't change his status*.

When a servant *fails, his whole position is at stake;* he might lose his job. When a child fails, he will be grieved because he has hurt his parents, and he will be corrected and disciplined. But *he is not afraid of being thrown out. His basic confidence is in belonging and being loved, and his performance does not change the stability of his position.*

Devadas and I read from Phillips' translation the thrilling words of Galatians 4:4-7,

When the proper time came God sent His Son, born of a human mother and born under the jurisdiction of the Law, that He might redeem those who were under the authority of the Law and lead us into becoming, by adoption, true sons of God. It is because you really are His sons that God has sent the Spirit of His Son into your hearts to cry, "Father, dear Father." You, my brother, are not a servant any longer; you are a *son*. And, if you are a son, then you are certainly an heir of God through Christ.

In the weeks to come Devadas told me that every time he found himself feeling and living as a servant, he would stop and once again remind himself, saying, "Father, dear Father, *I am Your son, and I'm going to live and feel like one!*"

Through the years I have seen this miracle of grace take place in many performance-bound Christians. I dare to believe it can happen in you.

Two.

BARRIERS TO GRACE

Thou great mysterious God unknown,
Whose love hath gently led me on,
Even from my infant days,
Mine inmost soul expose to view,
And tell me if I ever knew
Thy justifying grace.

Whate'er obstructs Thy pardoning love,
Or sin or righteousness, remove,
Thy glory to display,
Mine heart of unbelief convince
And now absolve me from my sins,
And take them all away.

The performance-based Christian life comes from the malignant virus of sinful pride—a pride which encourages us to build our lives upon a deadly lie. This lie claims that everything depends on what *we* do and on how well *we* perform, on *our* efforts and *our* work. We will enjoy acceptance and love if we can win them, success and status if we can earn them.

This pride extends to every area of life but is especially crucial to significant relationships, including our relationship to God (salvation), our relationship to ourselves (self-esteem), our relationship to other people (security and satisfaction from friendships, marriage, and parenthood), and our relationship to society (success and status). In other words, whether or not God loves us, or whether we can feel good about ourselves, or whether other people will like us, or whether we will be considered a success in life—all depends on how well we can perform. *Everything of importance in life is conditioned on whether we can deliver a perfect, or at least near-perfect, performance.*

Such prideful self-reliance is the very opposite of grace. I presume most Christians know by heart the common definition that grace is "the unmerited favor of God." Sometimes this is further clarified by the words, "freely bestowed upon the undeserving." Notice how the key phrases contradict what we've been describing.

Unmerited favor	vs.	Earned acceptance
Freely bestowed	vs.	Conditionally given
Undeserving receivers	vs.	Worthy achievers

By this time I can hear many of you protesting, "But that's old stuff. I know all that. Of course I believe in salvation by grace and *only* grace. Are you implying that I believe in some kind of salvation by works? Or a 'works righteousness'? I gave all that up when I accepted Christ as my Saviour, when I first became a Christian. I guess I'd have to admit I'm a lot like some of the people you described in the first chapter. But *this* couldn't possibly be the reason. Our church strongly preaches salvation by grace and I fully believe in it myself. I even witness about it to others."

I appreciate your sincerity but ask you to take a deeper look, for I've heard it too many times. You see, for almost twenty-five years it has been my privilege to counsel students and staff from Asbury College and Asbury Theological Seminary. These institutions are strongly evangelical in theology and very evangelistic in world outreach. Almost everyone who has come to me for counseling has had a sound biblical theology of grace. However, like the missionary mentioned in chapter 1, the deeper we counseled the more startled they were to discover it was "all in the head." Now it is better to have a right theology than a wrong one. But it isn't good enough. In fact it often proves a way of defending ourselves against the facts and thus failing to get in touch with the root of our problems.

Gut-Level Grace

A sound theology of grace can literally be purely *propositional* or all in the head, and not *visceral* or in the heart. We think the term *gut level* is fairly modern and realistic. But it's fascinating to remember that people in Bible times considered the stomach, the belly, as the source of deeply experienced beliefs and emotions. And so those passages which we translate with "heart," the older *King James Version* translates with "belly" and "bowels."

"Out of his belly shall flow rivers of living water" (John 7:38, KJV).

"If there be any consolation in Christ . . . any comfort . . . any bowels and mercies . . ." (Philippians 2:1, KJV).

"Yea, brother, let me have joy of thee in the Lord; refresh my bowels in the Lord" (Philemon 20, KJV).

"But whoso hath this world's good, and seeth his brother have need, and shutteth up his bowels of compassion from him, how dwelleth the love of God in Him?" (1 John 3:17, KJV)

In biblical days, the word *bowels* was used exactly as we use *gut level* now. Much more than mere emotions, it also included attitudes and actions and deeds, and was an all-pervasive way of thinking, feeling, doing, and relating. It meant that the whole personality was affected, right down to the deepest levels.

Today, many Christians have a sound biblical doctrine of grace to which they give full mental assent. It is a truth they *believe about* God, but it is not their gut-level basis of *living with* God, themselves, and others. It is *doctrinal* but not *relational*; it is believed *in* but not lived *out.*

Ted was an older seminary student who came to share some family problems with me. Typical of the many second-career men God seems to be calling into ministry these days, he was married and had teenage children. He had left a good job to obey God's call, after he and his wife experienced dramatic conversions from what he called "the fast lane of Yuppie sin." Now he commuted every weekend to pastor two rural churches. He studied hard and visited his parishioners faithfully. He forcefully preached the transforming grace of God, saw lives changed, and watched the churches grow.

Then his eldest daughter began to rebel against this new life. She changed her lifestyle—clothes, hairdo, friends, language, habits—the works, and became an embarrassment to him in the seminary community and in his pastorate. Ted was amazed at how much he was beginning to resent his daughter. He was also feeling some anger at God—how could He let this happen, when they had sacrificed so much to answer the call to service?

28

As we talked, I began to suggest that although God did not *cause* the situation, He did want Ted to *learn* from it, to begin to understand the pain that the Heavenly Father must have felt when Ted was living in sin. And, most of all, to understand what *love and grace* are all about. We talked and prayed together several times as Ted struggled with his feelings of anger and injustice. Slowly, he began to understand the cost of unconditional love and undeserved mercy—that God always accepts and loves us, even though He cannot approve of our behavior.

As Ted reached out to communicate grace to his daughter, he could see it was starting to make a difference in both of their lives. In our final time together, he was filled with deep emotion. "You know," he said, "I've studied about God's grace, I've believed it with all my heart, I've preached about it regularly, and seen several people wonderfully changed by it. But I can see that it's been mostly in my head. Now, God has allowed me to feel this kind of pain, because it's the only way He could shake grace loose from my head. It needed to be lowered about eighteen inches so I could experience it in my heart!"

You too may be saying, "That's exactly what I need. Like Ted, my theological and mental grasp of grace needs to penetrate into my innermost being and become gut-level grace. I want that desperately." Now if this is what you truly want, why is it so difficult? Why does it seem almost impossible to really live out grace on every level of life? Why do you cling tenaciously to patterns of performance that are totally unscriptural and that continue to make life so miserable?

At this point the easiest thing would be to go straight back to the Garden of Eden, talk about the results of the Fall and point out humanity's pride, self-centeredness, and rebellion against God. After all, isn't sin the fountainhead of this whole poisonous stream? Yes, but if we did that just now, I'm afraid it would be merely another head trip, one more interesting doctrinal excursion on a cognitive level which would not really produce change on a gut level. Unfortunately, this is what many pastors and counselors do and thereby miss the real problem—the deep-seated barriers to grace which have been implanted in many people. Of course, these barriers include ideas which operate in the conscious level of the personality. But they also include feelings, habits, attitudes and reactions, predispositions and presuppositions which have been conditioned by the memories and patterns of prior experiences and relationships. Most of these sensations operate from the deep subconscious level of the personality. They are not simply concepts or mental images. They are *feeling/concepts*, or *concept/feelings*, mental images so intertwined with emotions that each one affects the other. They need to be penetrated by the Gospel; in many instances, they require *healing grace* in addition to *a renewal of the mind*.

Cultural Barriers to Grace

In my other writings I have described how family life experiences and relationships can create in us badly distorted pictures of God.[1] In a similar way, some of the basic presumptions of a culture can affect our conceptions of grace. For most of the ideas in this section I am indebted to Ralph Satter, a graduate student in our E. Stanley Jones School of Missions and Evangelism. With his permission I am using material from his proposed doctoral thesis.[2]

Scholars who make a special study of other peoples and their cultures are called anthropologists. Their research has conclusively proved that the people of one country may have very different ways of looking at life and reality than people from another country. This distinctiveness is a *worldview*, a kind of mental map or way of looking at life which determines how a people lives. A worldview largely depends on the underlying beliefs, assumptions, and values which almost everyone takes for granted. People may not talk about them, question them, or even be aware of them. They are just "there."

In my sixteen years of missionary life in India, I was constantly running into the differences between an American and an Indian worldview which was predominantly Hindu. When I would preach on being born again, I was often misunderstood and thought to be talking about reincarnation or being born again and again and again. When the Russian leader Khrushchev visited India, he made a good impression. But later at the United Nations, he got angry, took off his shoe, and pounded the table with it. India was horrified! The Indian people associate footwear with dust and dirt, and "to slipper" someone is the greatest possible insult. And did you ever try to explain the germ theory of disease to someone who believes diseases are caused by angered spirits? Every seemingly rational argument you can use, "Germs are invisible," and "They get inside the body," only reinforces their worldview. They know the spirits are invisible and get inside the body!

A worldview is like a lens through which people see all of life. The lens in our glasses depends on the kind of refraction the optician has ground into them. In the same way, our worldview depends on the refraction of our basic ideas, ideals, and core values.

What, then, is our North American worldview? What does the Gospel look like through our cultural lens? Are there some underlying assumptions and values so deeply ingrained in the "American way of life" that they actually bend and distort the biblical understanding of salvation by grace? Are they so strong as to make it difficult for us to live by grace? Let's take a closer look at three elements of American culture which can be barriers to grace.

● Self-reliance. Most researchers would agree that self-reliance is a dominant cultural value in America. Compare, for example, an elderly American man who is dependent on his children for support with an elderly Chinese in a similar situation. The Chinese, whose society does not idealize self-reliance, is proud of his children and brags on how good they are to him. The American is ashamed and doesn't want anyone to know. Instead, he wants to boast of his independence from his children. He would rather get a loan from a bank than from a relative. He tends to apologize for bothering his friends when something breaks down.

Such self-reliance is quite contrary to grace, for grace is free for the asking; it is God-reliant, God-dependent. In the Christian life, extreme self-reliance makes us try to be our own saviors and sustainers. It's hard for Americans to think any good could come out of a dependent relationship, but that's what grace is all about. The ideal of self-sufficiency, deeply ingrained in most Americans, causes many Christians to take the very means of grace and put them on the performance treadmill. While they may use the language of grace, at a deep gut level, they live as if their salvation and security depend on how much they read or pray or give or work or witness.

● Individualism. This highly prized American value is best expressed in "doing your own thing." We are now seeing ridiculous extremes in the interpretation of the U.S. Constitution because of an excessive emphasis on individualism.

Individualism is the theme of many great American novelists, such as Ernest Hemmingway and others. In the 1985 bestseller, *Habits of the Heart: Individualism and Commitment in American Life*, Robert Bellah and his colleagues glorify various aspects of American individualism that make it possible for a person to get ahead on his own initiative, in the pursuit of wealth or self-expression. Interestingly enough, even "biblical individualism" is highlighted in the book.

While Scripture gives attention to the individual, this is balanced by an emphasis on God's actions of both love and judgment upon families, communities, and nations. In the New Testament, saving grace is always relational and is found only in the fellowship of Christ and His people. There are no Lone-Ranger Christians, and the term *saints* is never in the singular. Grace is received and lived out in the community of faith. The "whosoever wills" of Scripture are balanced with "you will be saved— you and your household" (Acts 16:31).

Too many people regard religion as one more avenue for self-discovery and self-realization, rather than receiving grace, allowing Christ to reign within, and living in a grace relationship with others. Salvation is a matter of being dependently related to Christ, who said, "Apart from Me you can do nothing."

• Activism. A number of cultural anthropologists have pointed to American activism as an optimistic view of effort. "You can do/be/get anything you really want to if you work hard enough. If at first you don't succeed, try, try again." Bellah observes that the demand to make something of yourself through work is a requirement Americans put upon themselves.

Certainly, doing and obeying are stressed throughout Scripture. We *are* to be "doers" as well as "hearers" of the Word (James 1:22). All manner of good works are enjoined upon us, but never as a way of winning or earning God's approval. Christ died for us while we were powerless—still sinners—long before we could do anything to achieve our salvation (Romans 5:6-8). Redemption is a pure gift of grace and involves receiving rather than achieving. Good works are the fruit of being accepted, not the cause of it. They are our response to God's unconditional love.

But Americans regard approval, success, and status as rewards for performing well. When this value system is translated into the Christian life, salvation becomes a matter of our efforts. A cartoon picturing modern-day Pharisees was captioned, "We get our righteousness the old-fashioned way—we *earn* it!" Americans have difficulty with grace!

Satter points out that one of the best serendipities of Evangelism Explosion training is that many of the volunteers come to truly experience grace for the first time in their lives. This may *happen years after the trainees have accepted Christ as their own Saviour!*

Because many aspects of the American cultural worldview have been exported, they are now shared by other countries of the world. For example, Devadas, in my opening story, was a third-generation Christian and very westernized in his outlook. In the swiftly developing countries of the world, many people experience such barriers to grace. While we rejoice in progress, we are saddened when we see some of the same hindrances to grace developing in those nations. The American rat race needs healing, not exporting.

What About the Church?

It is possible to argue that the church, the divinely instituted body of Christ, could not possibly be part of the problem. One could point out those times and places in history where the church has greatly influenced or shaped the culture around it, often achieving tremendous triumphs over evil. For example, it is generally conceded that the Wesleyan revival of the eighteenth century saved Britain from the chaos and carnage of an upheaval like the French Revolution. Many social reforms resulted from the tenacious efforts of evangelical Christians in Parliament, from the abolishment of slavery to a law requiring the painted line found on the side of ships which limited their loads. Formerly, the greedy owners overloaded ships and many lives were lost in storms at sea.

Truly "our citizenship is in heaven" (Philippians 3:20), and we are called to "not conform any more to the pattern of this world but to be transformed," and also certainly to transform society.

Furthermore, the church is one of the very agencies of grace. Traditional Roman Catholics would go further and say it is the *only* one and that saving grace comes through their particular church. But all such ideas fail to make an important distinction. The *church*, the universal and *invisible* body of Christ, made up of all persons who believe in Him as their true Saviour and Lord, is a divine and perfect *organism*. But *the visible church as we experience it, is a very human and imperfect organization*. As such it partakes of the fallenness and imperfections of human structures.

While every genuine believer is a vital part of the invisible body, it is the visible and local church with which we are concerned at this point. We must always remember that those who make up the visible church are products of a particular culture. So it shouldn't surprise us to discover within the church certain impediments to receiving and living out grace.

● The gospel of success. American activism has clearly infected the church's idea of success. The size and design of facilities, the amount of the annual budget, steady growth in membership, and numbers in attendance—these define a successful church or ministry. The health-and-wealth gospel proclaimed by many pastors and televangelists is the most extreme example of this. The name-it-and-claim-it variety shows that Christianity can literally be absorbed by the American worldview. No wonder the church is lampooned by secular comedians as promoting a blab-it-and-grab-it religion.

To those of us who have been missionaries among the poor and oppressed, this twisted version of the Gospel is shocking. When I think of thousands of faithful Indian Christians who own no land, and are thus at the economic mercy of unbelieving neighbors, and who sacrifice for their faith and struggle just to survive, I am appalled and angered when I hear this success-by-achievement gospel that can apply only to the affluent. I heard a sermon based on the New Testament story of the Rich Young Ruler that was given an incredible conclusion. You recall how the young man refused Jesus' challenge to give away his possessions, take up his cross, and follow Him. The televangelist accurately called him a millionaire, and then commented, "The poor fool! He didn't realize it, but if he had only obeyed Jesus and sacrificed his possessions, *Jesus would have made him a billionaire!*"

Certainly, most churches do not go to such extremes. But who can deny the emphasis on activity and the pressure of programming which is the accepted routine of the weekly church calendar? Or the minister's regular call for commitment to these activities to prove the depth of our Christian experience? Gradually we accept the inference that victorious Christian living depends on how well we perform in the church program. It's not hard to understand the average pastor's frustration. His responsibility is to keep things running and to raise the money to pay the bills and meet the denominational apportionments. When he sees this not happening because of the lack of commitment of his people, he tends to make commitment the theme of many sermons. As a result the people think that commitment and performance are what Christianity is all about. A kind of faith-commitment becomes the work by which they can be justified!

All this is a far cry from the true Gospel of undeserved and unearnable grace which alone can put us into a right relationship with God so that we can be "called children of God" (1 John 3:1). *God's grace makes us worthwhile and valuable for who we are, and not because of what we success-*

fully accomplish. I believe the church's distorted gospel of activism and self-effort contributes greatly to the self-belittling and low sense of self-worth so many people feel. It is also a main source of guilt and shame. We are somehow made to feel guilty if we have not succeeded in every area of life—church activities, job, marriage, parenthood—or in trying to relate to someone hardly anyone can get along with. This is implied even in those situations which are obviously not our fault or under our control. One example of this is the way many churches look down on divorced persons—regardless of the cause—as if they are moral lepers.

With the success-based "oughtness" of so many churches, it is easy to consider oneself a *failure.* This is equally as true for clergy as for laity. I've seen many a young pastor break under the stress of the local and denominational performance-demand and finally leave the ministry.

• The gospel of self-reliant individualism. Another aspect of the church's life which conflicts with biblical grace is an overemphasis on *the individual Christian life apart from open grace-filled relationships with other people.* The New Testament always presumes that if we *receive* God's unconditional acceptance and grace, then we will always *give* the same kind of grace to other people. But this means that the church should provide an atmosphere where this is possible. So many churches function like one more spectator sport with little or no genuine participation in relationships. Most of us are hesitant to let people get to know us; in church, we feel we always have to "put our best spiritual foot forward" and "keep our halos on straight." When this is combined with the success emphasis, most people are afraid and ashamed to share problems or weaknesses. Some close up from the sense of, "If I'm a Christian I ought to be able to handle it myself." This too contributes to these feelings of unreality and phoniness we have described.

In spite of years faithfully attending and working in the church, many persons never experience the changes that should come from grace. Their deepest needs are not only unmet, but they are not even uncovered. The tragedy is that this kind of sterile atmosphere drives Christians into greater hiding and reinforces their emotional and spiritual problems. They join the ranks of the disillusioned and the disheartened.

• The gospel of legalism. Legalism has always been a problem for the church. The belief that salvation comes through keeping commandments and rules is as old as humankind and is the one basic falsehood behind every religious system in the world—that we can earn God's approval and love by keeping certain moral laws.

Evangelical churches and pastors believe in and proclaim a doctrine of salvation by grace through faith, and would not intentionally propagate salvation by works. But the Sunday School lessons and sermons are sometimes not heard as messages of grace. Instead, the hearers filter them through our cultural and religious worldview and distort them into a contradictory gospel—a mixed message of grace and works, unconditional love and performance-based acceptance. Like all mixed messages, this one produces confusion which results in emotional and spiritual problems.

We have looked at some of the general aspects of life which are seldom considered as possible barriers to understanding and accepting grace. Now let us turn to the greatest hindrance of all—destructive interpersonal relationships within the home and family.

Three.

PARENTAL GRACE— OR DYSGRACE

Come, Father, Son and Holy Ghost,
To whom we for our children cry:
The good desired and wanted most
Out of thy richest grace supply;
The sacred discipline be given
To train and bring them up for heaven.

God uses many means to prepare us for our need of Christ as Saviour. One of these is *parental grace*, which is intended to be a gentle yet most effective means of grace. All through Scripture God made covenants with families. It was His intention that the children included in these covenants be brought up in the "training and instruction of the Lord" and thus be awakened to love and serve Him.

When I was a youngster, my parents often told me they had prayed for me long before I was born. I didn't like that at all. I felt it took unfair advantage of me as a little child and didn't seem to give me much choice. Later as I observed other families, I began to appreciate their prayers. Someone has reminded us that from the day we were born we were in debt—we owed for nine months room and board! This is true for all of us, but how much more for those from Christian homes!

Before we can see what a terrible barrier to grace the home can be, we need to look at it *positively*, from the viewpoint of what God intended parenting to be, in His scheme of preparatory grace.

At this point there are two ways we can go. We can look to the researched findings of psychology and the behavioral sciences (discovered truth) to provide us with the model of what a good home and proper parenting should be. Or we can look to Scripture (revealed truth) as our starting place and then later use the proven findings of developmental psychology to enlighten those principles. As an evangelical Christian, I am committed to Scripture as the primary source and the authority for judging all truth, and so we shall begin there.

Parental Grace in Jesus' Life
Let's look at the perfect family model, that which Jesus experienced. When the Son of God became incarnate in

the human life of Jesus of Nazareth, none of the laws of human growth and development were suspended or violated. God could and did bypass the normal reproductive processes in what we call the Virgin Birth, but that is a misleading term. What we really mean is the Virgin Conception. As the creeds state, Jesus was "conceived by the Holy Spirit." This was certainly a supernatural act, a miracle. *But from the moment of His conception, all the regular laws of human development were in operation.* Jesus was *conceived supernaturally* but, like all other human babies, He grew in His mother's womb and was *born naturally.*

In Philippians 2:6-8, Paul describes the deep *kenosis,* the emptying or humbling involved when our Lord gave up the glories of His divine equality and kingly prerogatives. But Jesus did not give up the necessity of a human home with a mother and a father who possessed the divinely designed qualities for good parenting. God Himself built into this world a family plan, a purpose for parenting and family which reflects His own character.

The Scripture goes out of its way to picture the Virgin Mary as a *woman* of special godliness, holiness, and obedience to God (Luke 1:26-55); and Joseph as a righteous *man* of integrity, stability, and obedience to God (Matthew 1:18-25). And it portrays them as a *married couple* with high priority for the spiritual values of life. Luke tells us the natural outcome of such a home: "And the Child grew and became strong; He was filled with wisdom, and the grace of God was upon Him" (Luke 2:40). With full respect to the uniqueness and the deity of Christ, I believe we can still say that the chief instrument of God's love *at this particular time in His life* was the parental grace of Mary and Joseph. Must we not conclude from this that God the Father had carefully provided the atmosphere in which the Son's *human spirit* would find its proper identity, security, and self-esteem?

This can come about only as a human being responds

during the important developmental years to unconditional acceptance, physical and emotional nurture, stability, love, and discipline. This requires parents of godly character who demonstrate righteousness, loving-kindness, and predictable graciousness. If we take the Nazareth family as our model, then we have to conclude that all deviations from that pattern in the direction of unrighteousness, instability, unlovingness, or indiscipline, create deprivation and distortion to the foundations of personality. Such damages become barriers to grace and cause emotional and spiritual problems which often erupt later on under the stresses of the performance-conditioned life.

Luke was an amazingly careful historian, dating events as you would expect a doctor to, with clinical precision. He recorded the events at Jerusalem, in the temple with Simeon and Anna, as taking place at "the time of their purification according to the Law of Moses" (Luke 2:22). That is, when Jesus was forty days old.

"When Joseph and Mary had done everything required by the Law of the Lord, they returned to Galilee to their own town of Nazareth. And the Child grew and became strong; He was filled with wisdom, and the grace of God was upon Him" (2:39-40). The word Luke used is *paidion,* meaning "little child." It is obvious that God's grace in these early developmental years came "upon" Jesus through the nurturing grace of His parents. The channel was clearly parental grace, and we can clearly trace its results to the twelve-year-old Jesus. "And He went down to Nazareth with them and was obedient to them. . . . And Jesus grew in wisdom and stature, and in favor with God and men" (Luke 2:51-52).

This is what God intended to be the model and pattern for all parental grace. Note the five areas of parental care and the corresponding personality development so clearly presented in God's Word.

- Physical. "The child grew and became strong"

(2:40). This reference is obviously to the infant Jesus. "And Jesus grew in . . . stature" (2:52) describes Him at the age of twelve. The most elemental part of parental grace is bodily nourishment and protection provided through the supply of basic needs. Though it is primarily physical, it is related to the total development of the person. Research among the famine children of Africa reveals permanent brain damage and impaired capacity for emotional expression as a result of physical deprivation. Here in America we are just beginning to understand the psychophysical consequences of underfed children from poor and deprived homes. We are also seeing what happens to those from affluent homes where tobacco, drugs, liquor, and excesses of sugar and junk foods are a regular part of their "nourishment." Either kind produces undernourished children who will suffer unhealthy consequences.

● Mental. Both Luke 2:40 and 2:52 describe Jesus as growing in wisdom. From a scriptural standpoint, this growth includes knowledge but goes much further. Wisdom is the art of reaching right ends by use of right means. It is giving to the things of God the same kind of dedication and intensity that people give to worldly affairs (Luke 16:8). Jesus' home provided the atmosphere and encouragement for full mental development; that is, a deep understanding of the Scriptures and their practical, down-to-earth application in daily living.

● Social/Relational. Jesus grew on the horizontal and interpersonal plane, "in favor with . . . men." It is obvious that Jesus had good personal relationships with other people. Being loved and cared for by parents creates a strong sense of security and belongingness which enables growing youngsters to reach out and relate to other people. The popular Gaither song expresses this truth very beautifully, "I am loved, I am loved, I can risk loving you." One of the first areas where we see the destructive effects of those deprived of parental grace is in their inability to build deep and lasting relationships with others.

• Personal/Volitional/Emotional. "Then He went down to Nazareth with them and was obedient to them" (2:51). This verse precedes the one which describes Jesus' growth and often gets left out of the list, when it is actually the foundation. Jesus had just expressed to His parents for the first time the growing realization of His true identity, by saying, "Didn't you know I had to be in My Father's house?" His parents "did not understand what He was saying to them" (2:49-50). In spite of His growing consciousness that God was His true Father, and the tension He felt because of His parents' lack of understanding, Jesus *deliberately chose to put Himself under their authority and be obedient to them.* One of the central purposes in parental grace is to teach obedience. A child needs to understand that genuine love provides limits, and that affection and discipline go together. Both are essential to healthy personality development. I have deliberately placed this just before the spiritual element. A child learning obedience and submission to the authority of parents is being prepared to surrender to the will of God. Such learning is at the heart of real maturity.

But this is not simply a matter of parents forcing obedience on their children. It is of tremendous importance to realize that the Apostle Paul carefully restated the fifth commandment in line with the spirit of the New Testament. He put part of the responsibility for the children's obedience squarely onto the attitude of the parents, so that attitude is an important manifestation of parental grace! The commands and regulations of parents need to be "in the Lord," in accordance with God's moral principles, and should be carried out in the proper spirit, so that their disciplining will not cause the children to become frustrated, exasperated, and resentful (Ephesians 6:1-4; Colossians 3:21). I shall be eternally grateful for this kind of parental grace which came to me, particularly through my father. He made it so much easier for me to believe in and surrender to my Heavenly Father.

• Spiritual/Relational. Jesus grew on the vertical plane, "in favor with God." This is the main purpose of being brought up "in the training and instruction of the Lord" (Ephesians 6:4). As John the Baptist was a forerunner of Christ, so parents too are to "prepare the way for the Lord and make straight paths for Him" (Matthew 3:3). Parental grace is intended to get the road ready for God's coming in saving grace.

Parental Dysgrace

Unfortunately, parents also have the power to strew boulders on the road and, indeed, be roadblocks instead of forerunners of saving grace. In order to describe this side of the picture I am using the term *dysgrace*, which is the tragic distortion of grace.

The prefix *dys* has an interesting history and use in our language.[1] It comes from the middle English, *dis*, which came from the Old French, and from the Latin, *dys*. They all have their root in an ancient Greek word, *dus*, which means bad or evil. *Dys* is commonly used in medically related words when something has gone wrong, where there is *disease* (dis-ease); *dyspepsia* (disturbed digestion, indigestion); *dyslexia* (impairment of reading ability); *dystrophy* as in muscular dystrophy (deterioration and atrophy of the muscles). It is most clearly understood in the word *dysfunction* which means the disordered or impaired functioning of any system. Thus, *dysgrace* is grace which has been distorted or impaired so that it does the opposite of what it was intended to do. *Grace* is constructive; *dysgrace* is destructive. *Grace* encourages life and produces healthy personality growth; *dysgrace* impairs life and produces malignant personality growth.

What happens when parental grace becomes parental dysgrace? What results when that which God intended to be the greatest instrument of growth and development becomes an instrument of impairment and dysfunction? The very opposite takes place. Instead of helping prepare a human being for the new birth and new life with God, parental dysgrace becomes an obstacle to the new birth. Why? The foundations for interpersonal relationships are laid in the early years of childhood. Just as there is a *physical womb* in which the unborn baby's biophysical life is nourished and nurtured, so there is *an emotional and spiritual womb* in which the young child's relational life develops. An infant learns a language of relationship before it learns to speak. Prompt attention to physical needs, unconditional acceptance and affection conveyed through holding and bonding, facial expressions and tones of voice showing approval and love—all communicate messages of grace. Deprivation, neglect, conditional acceptance based on perfect performance, unpredictable affection, rejection, condemning faces and angry voices communicate the very opposite. Grace then becomes distorted and dysfunctional to the child. In later years, if ungracious words and corresponding actions are added to this early atmosphere of dysgrace, the growing child begins to live out the dysgraceful pattern of relationships he has been experiencing.

The four most basic concepts of life grow out of the interpersonal relationships we experience during our developmental years. When I refer to a concept, as I often do in all my writings, I do *not* mean a purely mental image. I mean both the mental picture and the emotional content or feelings, which surround it. Since we are whole persons, these two always go together, whether we realize it or not. So when we use the word *concepts* we are actually talking about *concept/feelings* or *feeling/concepts* which ultimately become *all-persuasive personality patterns*. Let's look at these four life-determining concepts.

Your Concept of Self

The family is the chief source of how we see ourselves. This is so true that some have called it the "looking-glass self." At first a baby has no self-awareness. Around eighteen months of age, most children are able to distinguish themselves from others and have the rudiments of self-image. From then on their picture is enlarged until it becomes life-sized. It comes primarily from the reflections and the reactions to themselves by the persons closest to them. It is a concept/feeling about themselves. In this sense the home is like a *mirror* in which they see themselves. Their self-estimate will largely depend upon the worth, or worthlessness, reflected in the mirrors of the people who mean the most to them. Their audiovisual playbacks become the basis of how they will perceive themselves in years to come.

Jack was a young man whose friends described him as one who "had it all together." Successful in his work, happily married with an attractive family, he was well respected in both church and community. Then when he hit thirty-five things began to change—not on the outside, but within. In my counseling I long ago became aware of what I consider a kind of "young adult crisis" in the lives of many Christians. This usually takes place somewhere between the ages of twenty-six to thirty-eight. There are often several factors involved, like stresses related to marriage, parenting of children, financial needs, or relationships with parents and in-laws. However, the one which seems to bring these people for help is *the emergence, sometimes almost the eruption, of negative and destructive emotions.* These often represent the very opposite of who and what these persons think they are. This emergence is what had pushed Jack out of his comfortable life and led him to seek help. Before this he never understood my sermons on damaged emotions. and was a bit impatient with Christians who thought they needed counseling or healing.

At first Jack was embarrassed and puzzled. "All hell seems to have broken loose in my personality," he hesitantly confessed to me. I inquired about any possible physical factors. He assured me his recent, company-required checkup proved him to be "disgustingly healthy." When we surveyed possible situational factors, we came up with none. Slowly but surely it became clear—Jack seemed gripped with deep feelings of fear, insecurity, and self-doubt. In spite of all the successful realities to the contrary, he had an overwhelming sense he was a complete failure. This was so strong that he was also being tempted by certain desires and sins quite new to him, which added to a sense of spiritual failure. It became obvious that Jack had pushed a lot of hurtful things down into the basement of his personality. As he put it, "They seem to be coming up through the furnace ducts."

From his earliest years Jack felt he was neither wanted nor loved by his parents, particularly his father. "I never felt I was accepted or loved *for myself.* Only if I didn't cause any trouble or inconvenience for them, or if I brought them recognition or pride, or they could use me to advance their reputations—only then did they act like they even wanted me, let alone loved me. For years I just bulldozed over all those feelings and worked my way to success. I wouldn't let myself look at any of this because I couldn't stand facing the truth of it."

Jack fought back the hurt and tears. As he shared a kaleidoscope of recurring painful scenes, one particularly haunted him. He was only in kindergarten, and his mother was bringing him home from the hospital after some minor surgery. He felt nauseated and weak and she was helping him into the house. Dad was outside working on the car, his head down under the hood. Without even looking up, he had said in a disgusted tone, "All right now, don't come sniveling around me. I've got important work to do."

Jack had never received the life-giving nourishment of parental grace—Acceptance, Affection, and Affirmation. Now he was suffering from a case of "emotional vitamin A deficiency." He had been a victim of parental dysgrace which had left a huge hole at the center of his being and was disrupting the most important area in his life—his relationship with God. And that leads us to the second of these life-determining concepts.

Your Concept of God

The home is like a skylight through which we glimpse our first pictures of God. We get our earliest "feltness" of God through relating with our parents. A great many of their characteristics are woven into our idea of His character, from what is *caught* as well as *taught*. Few parents realize that whatever is *permitted* in the home is both taught and caught. I spend hours and hours with adults, some of them in later life, helping them reconstruct their concept/ feelings of God. Many of them have God and their parents all tangled up together. They need to get them separated before they can have a God fit to love and to live with.

While I could give scores of illustrations of horrible concepts of God which have their source in parental dysgrace, I would like us to look instead at the lifelong effect of parental grace which forms a good concept of God.

What a privilege it was to have Corrie ten Boom stay in our home for three days in 1961. She was speaking in a series of meetings at our church in Bangalore, India. (Incidentally, the things she enjoyed most were our ample supply of hot water and the thick American bath towels we provided for her!) I've never forgotten the stories she shared, as she paid tribute to the important role her home played in giving her the security and strength to withstand those terrible Holocaust prison experiences. Later I discovered she had summarized this in one of her books.

My security was assured in many ways as a child. Every night I would go to the door of my room in my nightie and call out, "Papa, I'm ready for bed." He would come to my room and pray with me before I went to sleep. I can always remember that he took time with us and would tuck the blankets around my shoulders very carefully, with his own characteristic precision. Then he would put his hand gently on my face and say, "Sleep well, Corrie . . . I love you."

I would be very, very still, because I thought that if I moved I might somehow lose the touch of his hand; I wanted to feel it until I fell asleep.

Many years later in a concentration camp in Germany, I sometimes remembered the feeling of my father's hand on my face. When I was lying beside Betsie on a wretched, dirty mattress in that dehumanizing prison, I would say, "O Lord, let me feel Your hand upon me . . . may I creep under the shadow of Your wings."

In the midst of that suffering was my Heavenly Father's security.[2]

Your Concept of Others

Our family relationships greatly affect the way we look at and relate to other persons. Do we see them as friends, competitors, antagonists, or perhaps even enemies? Do we expect others to treat us with respect or disdain? Are they out to help or to hinder? To lift us up or to let us down?

Do we live by the Golden Rule, or do we "do unto others before they do unto us"?

The home is like a *window* through which we look at others. It affects the way we see them and the way we think they see us. What *we* think *they* think of us has a great deal to do with how we expect them to relate to us. What makes the difference is whether we have received parental grace—or dysgrace.

Dr. Ken Magid is a practicing clinical psychologist and professor who teaches physicians in a medical school. He has recently written a book called *High Risk: Children Without Conscience.*[3] His main thesis is that America is in a "bonding crisis." This means that we are raising a whole generation of children who are victims of "the unattached child syndrome." They have never been truly "bonded" with their parents and, unless this is healed and changed, they will never get close to anyone. Because of parental behavior—what we have been calling parental dysgrace— he feels these children will grow into adults who do not seem to have a conscience and who are unable to genuinely relate to other people. Dr. Magid describes them as "trust bandits," the con artists of society, pathological liars, and in some instances dangerous criminals. At the core of their lives is a deep-seated rage born of their unfulfilled needs. It seems to be locked in their souls because of the emotional abandonment they experienced as children. Dr. Magid says it's as if a voice inside them says, "I trusted you to be there and to take care of me and you weren't. It hurts so much that I will not trust anyone, ever. I must control everything—and everybody—to ward off being abandoned again."[4] His book is filled with illustrations of many such persons so badly damaged by their homes that they have a difficult time ever receiving or giving love to others.

I am glad that we can have a more optimistic viewpoint because of the transforming power of Christ. Truly, "hope does not disappoint us, because God has poured out His love into our hearts by the Holy Spirit, whom He has given us" (Romans 5:5). But there are many people so badly scarred by the kind of damage Dr. Magid describes that deep healing grace is necessary to bring wholeness into their relationships with others.

Your Concept of Reality

Family is *the door* to the world. Since doors open both ways, how a child will experience life depends largely on the parents' interpretation of what comes in and what goes out of the home. That great passage on the home, Deuteronomy 6, stresses the importance of constant factual and moral instruction. The great principles of life are to be discussed with and lived out before children at every opportunity; when walking, talking, before retiring at night and upon arising in the morning (v. 7). They are to be the lifestyle of the home, woven into the very fabric of the family and becoming the symbols for all of life (v. 8). They are to be written on the doorways and the gates (v. 9). *Parents are truly God's doorkeepers.* Everything that goes in and out of the home is processed by their interpretation of life.

The truth of this was borne out some years ago when several outstanding persons were asked what most affected the forming of their moral standards for practical daily living. The majority replied it was the family conversation at mealtime. Through our homes we receive our concept of the world, life, reality itself, and how it all relates to some built-in principles we will be describing later on. This is why the *spoiled child* can have as many emotional and spiritual problems as the *abused child,* for there is just as faulty an idea of the world and life. Cruelty and abuse certainly distort right concepts, but so do affection without discipline and love without limits.

Earl Jabay, chaplain at the New Jersey Neuro-Psychiatric Institute at Princeton, has spent a lifetime working with alcoholics, drug addicts, and neurotic patients. He says one of their main problems is an improper view of reality and life. They think they can create a fantasy world of their own, make their own laws, and live their own lives accordingly. He uses this idea as titles for his books, *The God Players*, and *The Kingdom of the Self*.[5]

These are the four most important concept/feelings in our lives: those of ourselves, of God, of others, and of the world around us. And a significant part of their formation comes through the relationships we had with our parents. It remains to be seen in what way these life-determining concepts *help* or *hinder* us in living a life of grace.

Four.

HOW IT ALL BEGAN

My Saviour bids me come, Ah! why do I delay?
He calls the weary sinner home and yet from Him I stay.

What is it keeps me back, from which I cannot part?
Which will not let my Saviour take possession of my heart?

Some cursed thing unknown must surely lurk within;
Some idol, which I will not own, some secret bosom-sin.

Jesus, the hindrance show which I have feared to see;
Yet let me now consent to know what keeps me out of Thee.

W e've looked at several hindrances to grace which contribute to performance-style Christianity. Now, as we go behind these and see what causes them in the first place, we come to the heart of the problem—*sin*. According to the Bible, sin is both the *root* of what we've described as a malignant disease, and the *reason* why perfect performance can never cure it. *The heart of the problem is the problem of the heart*—fallen, diseased, and powerless to change itself.

But what's wrong with attempting perfect performance anyhow? We all want things to be perfect. The basic wrong with the attempt is that we no longer have that option. We lost it and can no longer speak of anything being truly perfect in this imperfect world. Obviously the key phrase there is "in this imperfect world." Does that mean it once was perfect? Yes, but it has fallen from the way it was, and so biblical Christians speak of a *fallen and imperfect world.* Something happened which destroyed its perfection. Does that mean life can never be fully perfect again? That's right, at least not here on this planet, and in the sense it originally was. Someday, certainly, but that will require "a new heaven and a new earth" (Revelation 21:1). Here and now, life can be perfect only in a new and different sense, in the way of God's freely given grace.

But we are getting ahead of ourselves. If we are to truly understand everything that is to follow, we must go back to the beginning. That's what Jesus did when He was questioned about the obvious difference between God's ideal plan (in this case, for marriage) and the less-than-ideal way it sometimes turns out to be in this fallen world. He said, "It was not this way from the beginning" (Matthew 19:8). Let's follow Jesus' example and go back to Creation. Interestingly enough, as I wrote this I began leafing through my copy of the *New International Version.* In turning to Genesis 1, I went back three pages too far

56

and found myself reading these words in the Preface. "Like all translations of the Bible, *made as they are by imperfect man, this one undoubtedly falls short of its goals.* Yet we are grateful to God for the extent to which He has enabled us to realize these goals and for the strength He has given us and our colleagues to complete our task." Amazing! Not even our Bible translations can escape the consequences of a fallen and imperfect world.

The Perfect Creation

The ancient philosophers used to argue about where humans got the idea of perfection. It couldn't have come from actual observation or experience, since nothing in this world is perfect. How then did they imagine a straight line or a perfect circle, when there really were no such things? Where did such ideas come from? And so they argued back and forth.

We Christians know that the idea of the perfect comes from a *perfect* God who created a *perfect* world with *perfect* humans made in His *perfect* image. At every step of the Creation process, God declared it to be good (Genesis 1:11, 18, 21, and 24). Finally, when He had created humankind in His own image, male and female, "God saw all that He had made and it was very good" (1:31). You notice it wasn't until God created beings in His own image that He considered it *very* good.

James, in his letter, adds the important word "perfect" to describe God's created gifts. "Every good and perfect gift is from above, coming down from the Father of heavenly lights" (1:17). Think now of how completely perfect God's very good creation really was. It is described in the first two chapters of Genesis.

• God made a perfect universe governed by perfect laws—*universal perfection.* Genesis 1:1-9, 14-18 describes the creation of the heavens and earth—light, the sky, the land; the seas, vegetation; the sun, moon and planets; all living creatures with provision for their maintenance.

- God made a perfect world of plants and animals with a perfect balance between them—*ecological perfection.* Genesis 1:11-13, 20-25, and 30 describe the way God provided food and sustenance for every level of His creation.

- God made a perfect man and a perfect woman with perfect gender identity and sexual orientation—*psychophysical perfection.* "Male and female He created them" (Genesis 1:26).

- God gave them perfect personalities, modeled after His own, minds with incredible powers to learn, and emotions with a strong sense of identity and a secure self-esteem. All this was so that the man and woman would have dominion over creation—*mental, emotional, and organizational perfection.* "God blessed them and said to them, 'Be fruitful and increase in number; fill the earth and subdue it. Rule over the fish of the sea and the birds of the air and over every living creature that moves on the ground" (Genesis 1:28).

- God gave them perfect companionship with one another, modeled after the harmony of His own social nature in which Father, Son, and Holy Spirit live in perfect unity and love—*relational perfection.* This meant perfect oneness and openness, with no defenses, no guilt, shame, or inhibitions. Think of it—nothing to hide! Adam and Eve had the capacity for perfect spiritual, emotional, and physical (sexual) union (Genesis 2:18-35). Verses 24-25 imply far more than the purely physical; they infer there were no barriers of any kind—mental, spiritual, emotional, or physical. "They will become one flesh. The man and his wife were both naked, and they felt no shame."

- God gave them a perfect fellowship with Himself—*spiritual perfection.* Genesis 3:8 describes what was intended to be a beautiful and natural relation of friendship between God and humans. It is the incredible picture of the Creator-Father who walks and talks with His children. "Then the man and his wife heard the sound of the Lord God as He was walking in the garden in the cool of the day."

This was the capstone of creation. God had provided *perfect fulfillment* through His *perfect design* for all the basic needs which He Himself implanted in the human personality. His design was not only perfect, but perfectly natural in the sense that it functioned *naturally*. Every thing and every animal and every human operated perfectly within the scheme that flowed out of their created natures. No one had to work at it in order to achieve it. If they lived according to the perfect divine plan and the perfect divine principles, all would function perfectly. Psalm 8:4-6 expresses it the best:

What is man that You are mindful of him? . . .
You have made him a little lower than God
And crowned him with glory and honor.
You have made him rule over the works of Your hands;
And put everything under his feet.

HUMANS

under

GOD

rooted in, but above

NATURE

Humans are under God, and rooted in, but above, Nature. This was the perfectly designed scheme. If the first humans would live accordingly, everything would be perfect. Ah, but that was a big *if*. And here was the one great difference between Adam and Eve and all of the creation below them. Things, plants, or animals fulfilled their purpose without having to make a choice. Their destiny had been fixed for them. But humans could accomplish their purposes only by choosing to stay *in the right relationship with their Creator*. And choice meant there was always the possibility of choosing not to do so. The various biblical words for sin express this—"crossing a line," "missing the mark," and "falling short."

The Fall
The Book of Genesis records the story of humanity's wrong choice and the terrible consequences which followed. We call it the Fall.

Humans, created to live *over and above* all other creatures, but *under* God, listened to the voice of the Evil One. Satan, one of the greatest of all the angels, had fallen from the heights of perfection, perhaps eons ago. This is described in Isaiah 14:12-15 and Luke 10:18. He desired to be as God himself, refused to accept his place, and fell to the bottom of the universe.

He sowed the deadly seeds of temptation in Adam's and Eve's minds until they began to question the goodness of God's character. They no longer saw God's loving limitation, "You must not eat from the (one) tree . . ." as the Father's gracious provision for His children to enjoy even more fully all the other trees in the garden. Instead, they were misled to perceive the limitation as the cruel prohibition of a malicious tyrant. And they chose not to accept God's word on the matter, but to do it their own way.

Even at this point there was no question of choosing good or evil, right or wrong—not in the sense, at least, in which we use those words now. Adam and Eve had only to live in childlike faith. They didn't have to make decisions of good or evil, right or wrong—they didn't even know what those words meant. Their only decision was between two opposing alternatives—to trust and obey God's word or to distrust Him and decide for themselves. Either they continued to live in a trusting, receiving relationship with God and thus to enjoy all His perfect gifts; or they refused to stay in that openhanded, obedient position, and taking matters in their own hands would begin to make decisions on the basis of what they felt was best.

Unfortunately, they rebelled against God and His way. They refused to accept the limitations of their humanity. They wanted to keep their position of being *above* nature, without being *under* God. They had perfection—being a little less than God Himself—but they wanted even more. They wanted to be *like* God, in the sense of being equal with Him (Genesis 3:4). Augustine put it this way:

> And what is the origin of our evil will but pride? For 'pride is the beginning of sin' (Ecclesiastes 10:13). And what is pride but the craving for undue exaltation? And this is undue exaltation, when the soul abandons Him to whom it ought to cleave as its end, and becomes a kind of end in itself.[1]

But when they tried to be *like* God, they not only failed to become *more* than they were, but actually became *less*. They could not achieve the glory and perfection that belongs only to God. Instead, they lost the only kind of perfection they had—a gift granted to them as beings created in God's likeness.

An Imperfect World

Because of the Fall, *imperfectness permeates the whole universe.* Try to grasp the all-inclusive losses which came about. The original and innate human perfections are gone, and we can never again regain them through our efforts, no matter how hard we try. But performance-oriented Christians find this hard to accept and go on living as if they can. "If only . . . if only we do well enough. If only someone else works harder. If only people would understand. . . . If only God would do something about it. After all, it ought to be, so it could be, it would be, if only. . . ."

In contrast to the performance *fantasy* many try to live by, let's look at what we lost in the Fall.

• We lost natural and ecological perfection. Romans 8:19-22 describes how "the whole creation" is now imperfect, groaning "as in the pains of childbirth," awaiting the day when it "will be liberated from its bondage and decay." One has but to look at the destructive list of natural evils, like earthquakes, storms, floods, tornadoes, volcanic eruptions, to see the out-of-balancedness of the natural world. *Chaos* has now entered into the *cosmos*. This doesn't mean that natural laws don't still operate; they do function, but the system is no longer perfect. One of the ways we humans still try to subdue and rule over nature is to better understand those laws, cooperate with them, and protect ourselves from natural destruction. Contemporary knowledge of ecology, weather forecasting, storm and earthquake warning, etc., is an example of trying to work with nature. However, the devastation, suffering, and death these natural evils bring are indiscriminate. They seem capricious and unjust. Insurance companies classify them as "acts of God," which is trying to explain one mystery by positing another. In counseling I have discovered that much of the anger in some Christians is because they just can't face the fact this is a fallen, imperfect, and often unfair world. They are plagued with much too high a sense of injustice, and this keeps them angry at life in general.

• We lost physical perfection. Myriads of everyday facts remind us of this painful reality—injury and suffering, disease and deformities, deterioration and death. We presume that if our first parents had not fallen, they would have passed on to their children and succeeding generations a perfect biophysical inheritance. Instead, we are all victims of a gene pool which gets increasingly imperfect, as physical, mental, and hormonal defects are passed from one generation to another. Many of these have a direct effect on our inborn temperaments and the kinds of infirmities we inherit or develop. Although these defects are not in themselves sinful, they are places of weakness which make us more vulnerable to certain temptations and thus more liable to sin. The inherited tendency toward being nervous and high-strung or toward certain types of depression are common examples of these weaknesses. One of the most difficult tasks in counseling performance-minded Christians is to help them accept their limitations and live within them.

• We lost mental perfection. We can only surmise at humankind's original mental powers. Certainly Adam's ability to instantly and intuitively class and name "each living creature" implies a kind of *direct and perfect knowledge* which we no longer possess. What he seems to have immediately apprehended comes to us only through long and laborious study.

Occasionally, in a Michelangelo or a Mozart, a Newton or an Einstein, we get a slight hint of humanity's original mental capacity. We call such a person a genius, which means we acknowledge what they have received to be a gift, and not only something they have achieved. While such rare exceptions remind us of what we lost in the Fall, we still don't mean that they are *perfect.* In the summer of 1987, newspapers carried the story of a brilliant young math student who discovered that even the great Isaac Newton had made a serious error in using the mathematical tables, following his discovery of the law of gravity. But we don't need such a spectacular proof of human imperfection. Our own daily experiences run the gamut from an embarrassing overdraft at the bank to a tragic highway death due to an error in judgment.

I am often amazed at the incredible assumptions some performance-minded and perfectionistic Christians live with. I listened to Angela tell me all the things for which she felt guilty. Her list got longer and longer, and she became very emotional as she heaped failure after failure on herself. Lines of strain showed on her face. It was obvious she was, as she put it, "living on the nub."

The more we talked, the deeper she dug herself into a quagmire of depression. I had to do something to break the melancholy spell. I leaned forward and said eagerly, "Angela, may I touch you?"

She looked startled and backed away from me. "What?"

Again I asked her, "May I touch you? You see, it's been a long time since I've seen such a divine being."

"What do you mean?"

"What I mean, Angela, is that only some kind of god-like creature could expect to do all the things you listed, let alone do them perfectly. You have absolutely divine expectations. Where did you ever get the notion that you or anyone else were expected to do all those things? What I hear you saying is you feel guilty because you can't do *everything and do it flawlessly.*"

Angela sat silent for quite a while. Then she hung her head and cried quietly.

"Do you know what I'm thinking?" she asked. "It's crazy and I'm ashamed to tell you. But this confirms what has been dawning on me lately. Somewhere a long time ago, I began to take seriously what my folks used to call me, 'Angel.' I can't believe it. I felt they expected so much of me that I began to play the part of an angel. I can't put all the blame on them—I brought a lot of this on myself, trying to feel special."

It was a Spirit-revealed moment of self-awareness which started Angela on a new pilgrimage of grace and freedom from the performance trap.

• We lost emotional perfection. There's no need to labor this point. All we have to do is to take an honest look in the mirror and see the vast array of our negative emotions—fear, worry, anger, rage, jealousy, and self-despising. Or to remember how unpredictable and uncontrollable is the range of feelings we often express, even toward those whom we love.

• We lost relational perfection. Perhaps this is the area where our emotional out-of-balancedness affects us the most. The beautiful openness and transparency which characterized Adam and Eve in Genesis 2:24-25 is gone. Now we are equipped with automatic defense mechanisms behind which we hide our true selves. We are *afraid* to bare ourselves emotionally and let ourselves be known by those close to us.

Often we are *ashamed* of our sexuality, even within marriage. Meaningful friendship, companionship, Christian fellowship, or the deeper intimacies of sexual oneness within marriage do not come about easily and naturally. They require a lot of effort—sometimes even pain. At best, they are not perfect; at worst, they can be terribly destructive.

• We lost spiritual perfection. This is the fundamental loss from which all the others come. Our *God-centeredness* has now become *self-centeredness*. What was originally a *perfectly unified and integrated self* is now *divided and imbalanced*. The human personality, once in *perfect harmony* with God, nature, others, and itself, is now *in conflict* with every one of these.

We have defaced what God created and intended to be called "son." The center has been displaced with an "I" so it spells "sin." What was perfect is fallen, bent, and broken. When you compare the thrilling beauty of Genesis 1–2 with the chilling wreckage of Genesis 3, you are struck by the terrible losses we have suffered.

No Way Back?

The worst of it is that there is no way back. "So the Lord God banished him from the Garden of Eden to work the ground from which he had been taken. After He drove the man out, He placed on the east side of the Garden of Eden cherubim and a flaming sword flashing back and forth to guard the way to the tree of life" (Genesis 3:23-24). *There is no way back to the kind of perfection the Garden of Eden represents. We have lost not only the perfect, but also our ability to earn, perform, or retrieve the perfect.* We truly live in *Paradise Lost.* There's no way back.

But we have not lost our *memory* of paradise, or our *need or desire for* it. God left the longing for the perfect within us. This longing is one of the basic hungers which characterize humans—like the hunger for food, security, belongingness, affirmation, affection, sex, and, above all, the need to love and be loved. The drive for perfection and the perfect is a vital part of our need for God. This gnawing nostalgia for perfection is an integral part of the God-shaped blank within us which *only God (the truly perfect) can fulfill.*

There's nothing wrong with this desire for perfection. Sin enters when we, as fallen creatures, insist on *defining perfection on our own terms and seeking it in our own way.* The drive to do this is at the very core of our fallen sinfulness. This *twisted self-centered pride which is the basis of performance-based Christianity* is indicted in Scripture as a "works" salvation, or, as Paul puts it, an attempt to be "justified by the law" (Romans 3:20). Let us summarize our desire for perfection with these opposites:

A virtue becomes a vice.

An ideal is turned into an idol.

A reality becomes a counterfeit.

A gift to be received we try to achieve.

The search for excellence twists into a struggle for supremacy.

An undeserved relationship distorts into deserved one-upmanship.

The empty, open hand becomes a grasping, clenched fist.

I have gone into considerable detail to explain the biblical basis for our perverted pursuit of perfect performance. It is rooted in "original sin," and is one manifestation of it. In some Christians, however, damaged emotions are so intertwined with sins of the spirit that special healing and reprogramming are necessary. While it is true that all of us are responsible for *our own sins*, there are many people who are also *victims of other people's sins*. Sometimes it is difficult to get these two sorted out properly. Many people will never find freedom from the performance trap and all the emotional and spiritual problems that go along with it until they do. This is why the Holy Spirit (the Great Counselor) often needs the help of a temporary human assistant. This is why healing grace usually comes only with the help of a pastor, a trusted friend, or a professional counselor. We will be looking into these aspects of the problem in later chapters.

But at this point it is important to see that the roots of performance orientation are theological. If the ultimate cure is grace, then the ultimate cause of the behavior is the failure to understand, experience, and live out grace at every level of our lives. This means we must learn to give up every futile attempt to achieve right relationships by any other means than God's total plan of grace. Until we do this we are doomed to be *Christian POWs.* Prisoners of War? No. *Performance Oriented Workers* and *Prisoners of Works.*

Claire, a Modern Samson

Do you remember the lady in chapter 1 who ended her letter, "I thought I had to earn His love and that caused me to almost take my life"? She is a homemaker named Claire who in desperation had attempted to end her life. However, like many others, she admitted that she had hoped she wouldn't succeed; it was really a desperate cry for help.

Claire used a biblical picture of herself that had never occurred to me. She said that before her suicide attempt she had deeply identified with Samson in the Old Testament. Here is the picture she was referring to. "Then the Philistines seized him, gouged out his eyes, and took him down to Gaza. Binding him with bronze shackles, they set him to grinding in the prison" (Judges 16:21). Claire said she felt just like that—as if she were in a prison, strapped to a great grindstone, turning around and around, almost like a chained animal. "I felt as if I was consigned to a treadmill. Whatever I tried took me in a vicious circle. Sometimes I could keep it under control and run slowly. But usually I'd get going faster and faster, because I felt driven to keep up. That is, to feel I was doing enough. But I never was, and so never felt accepted or acceptable. I was trapped and couldn't find a way to get off. I got more and more worn out. I can understand why Samson ended up pulling the whole thing down. There didn't seem to be any way out . . . even today I wonder."

I've heard this kind of a desperate cry from many a sincere child of God who is "sick and tired of being sick and tired." That day I shared with Claire some words conveying the strongest possible assurance of hope, words that fit so well her Samson picture, and spoken by Jesus as He began His ministry in the synagogue at Nazareth.

The Spirit of the Lord is on Me,
because He has annointed Me

to preach good news to the poor.
He has sent Me to proclaim freedom for the prisoners
and recovery of sight for the blind,
to release the oppressed,
to proclaim the year of the Lord's favor
(Luke 4:18-19).

The *New English Bible* renders this, "to proclaim release for prisoners . . . to let the broken victims go free." My prayer is the good news of the Gospel of Grace—the Lord's favor—may become a reality in your life.

Five.

THE BAD NEWS

Sinners, turn; why will you die?
God your Saviour asks you why;
God, who did your souls retrieve,
Died Himself, that you might live.

Will you let Him die in vain?
Crucify your Lord again?
Why, you ransomed sinners, why?
Will you slight His grace, and die?

I 'll never forget the first time I saw the Grand Canyon of Arizona. I was an MK (missionary's kid) who had seen many of the so-called wonders of the world. I had learned the hard way that the reality of sightseeing rarely lived up to the fantasy surrounding its advertising. So by the age of twelve I had already developed the practical philosophy of, "Don't get too excited about a famous sight, because it's not going to live up to your expectations."

It was in that skeptical spirit I approached the Grand Canyon in 1934. In those relatively uncommercialized days, you simply walked toward it and suddenly, there it was before you. I was shocked speechless and stood for a long time in sheer disbelief at the utter vastness of its size—the width, the breadth, the height of the chasm with that tiny ribbon of a river at the bottom—and the incredible spectrum of changing colors. It took several minutes to actually take it all in, to realize it was true. For the first time in my life the experience of something actually surpassed my expectations!

That's the picture which comes to my mind when I think of another chasm, greater even than the Grand Canyon—the chasm which exists between a perfect, holy God and imperfect, sinful human beings. It is a moral Grand Canyon and even more vast and unbridgeable. How can we get across this abyss? How can we bridge the gap? The truth is that we cannot, and this leaves us in an impossible predicament. God's Word makes it plain there is no way to negotiate a reconciliation from our side of the chasm. If it's ever to be bridged, it must be done from God's side. There is nothing we humans can do to meet the requirements of God's perfect law. Make no mistake about it—those requirements have not changed. His purpose for us is the same. He made us to live in perfect relationship with Himself and others, and He still wills our complete perfection.

Law and Love

When we talk in terms of love and law, we are not referring to do's and don'ts or a set of laws. People think
immediately of the Ten Commandments, the laws of the
Old Testament, or the commandments of the New. But it
was Jesus Himself who told us what the law really was, as
He restated an Old Testament injunction from Deuteronomy 6:5, "Love the Lord your God with all your heart and
with all your soul and with all your mind. This is the first
and greatest commandment. And the second is like it:
Love your neighbor as yourself. All the Law and Prophets
hang on these two commandments" (Matthew 22:37-40).
Building upon Jesus' words, Paul wrote, "Love is the fulfillment of the law" (Romans 13:8-10). The Apostle John
also emphasized love for God and others in 1 John 3:11-
24, and 4:7-21. There is no doubt that the *law of love* is
the center around which all the commands and prohibi-
tions of Scripture revolve, and the principle which gives
them their meaning.

To make matters even more impossible for us, God
requires His law to be kept perfectly *from our hearts.* Our
obedience must be *an inside job and not mere external con-
formity.* So it's not enough to avoid murder, adultery, or
stealing, for the commandments are now highly internalized. We are required not to resent, nor to be lustful, nor
to desire covetously. In the New Testament we learn that
we are to love God with all our hearts, forgive people from
our hearts, and do the will of God from our hearts (Matthew 22:37; 18:35; Ephesians 6:6).

This was the point behind Jesus' running battles with
the Pharisees, the performance-oriented workers of His
day. They kept the *letter* of the law perfectly but broke its
spirit constantly. Jesus said to them, "You hypocrites! Isaiah was right when he prophesied about you: 'These people honor Me with their lips, but their hearts are far from
Me. They worship Me in vain; their teachings are but

rules taught by men' " (Matthew 15:7-9, quoting Isaiah 29:13).

When we look at God's requirements of us from the inside out, it doesn't take long to see our impossible predicament—the chasm *between His requirements and our achievements, the great gulf between the ought and the is.* In the Fall not only did we create the chasm, but we lost the power to leap across it. Now that doesn't mean we don't try, for we do. We attempt to bridge the gap in ways old and new, all equally unsuccessful.

The Sloppy Agape Way

Agape is a Greek word for love that refers to God's love or to the kind of love God puts into our hearts. Sloppy agape is a sentimentalized version of God's love which is so out of balance it excludes all the other aspects of God's nature. It is a favorite in many modern religious circles, some of which even call themselves Christian. It simply denies there is a chasm by claiming that God is so loving He overlooks our sins and failures. This sloppy agape is like a thick syrup poured into the Grand Canyon, filling it right up to the top, so that you can't see any gulf between the two sides.

Or, it may say no chasm exists because there are no real differences between good and evil, right and wrong, truth and error, sin and righteousness. There are no moral distinctions, because everything is a part of God and is therefore good. Though some things may look evil to us, this is just an illusion.

This philosophy comes in several attractive packages. There is the kind popularized by celebrities on television, or in books and expensive seminars. It is an incredible sight to see someone on a TV talk show, who you know is living by alley-cat morals, saying "I am God!" Such claims are common to the New Age Movement. Those of us who have served as missionaries in India or the Far East recognize it as an emptyheaded and Americanized version of a very *old* Hinduism or Buddhism. There are other popular versions which reduce God to some kind of impersonal entity. Their benediction is, "May the force be with you."

Then there is a watered-down god of liberal Christians, who is so all-inclusive he is pictured as a kind of great-grandfather in heaven, a benevolent, simpleminded deity who smiles down at his creatures and says, "That's okay, just as long as the kids are having a good time."

The Bible makes plain that God's love is holy love. The same Apostle John who tells us, "God is love" (1 John 4:16) also declares, "God is light; in Him is no darkness at all" (1 John 1:5). There are scores of references in Scripture to the "wrath of God." Since we no longer use the word *wrath* very much, let us call it the anger of God. I realize this phrase creates a major problem with some Christians, many of whom are tender, supersensitive persons with warped and fearful concepts of God. Regardless of their good mental theology, at a gut level they feel God is an omnipotent heavenly ogre out to get them, and so are terrified. This is an area where we need some balanced biblical understanding of a very important truth, so let's face it head-on.

The anger of God simply means that God's holy nature is unalterably opposed to all sin. It means God cannot overlook sin or come to terms with it by making some kind of deal. Put simply, God is against all sin, in any form, anywhere, and at any time. Sin creates a disturbance in the moral order of the world which God cannot ignore. He cannot treat good and evil alike; to do so would be to deny His own moral nature.

The anger of God does not mean what anger often means to us—a fit of temper, an unpredictable emotion, a reaction of irritated self-concern accompanied by a loss of self-control. God does not have an outburst of temper against someone because of sin and then think of ways to get even. Rather, *God's anger is His predictable, steadfast antagonism toward anything sinful or unholy.*

We become further confused if we get anger and hate mixed up, since they are not the same. Parents know this. We can be very angry at our children and love them deeply *at the same time.* In fact, good parents take it a step further, so that there are times when our very anger proves how much we do love our children. For when we truly love them, we will not tolerate anything which would harm or destroy them, either from the outside or from within. The anger of God, His holy antagonism against sin, is sure proof of His redemptive concern for His children. God loves and cares for us so deeply that He is infinitely concerned about what happens to us.

"But," someone continues to protest, "I don't understand this anger of God business—it scares me." Maybe it will help if we ask, What is the alternative to the anger of God? The alternative is not a God of love, because, as we have seen, love and anger are two sides of the same coin, and you can't have one without the other. The alternative to anger is *apathy, which would mean an apathetic God who is morally neutral and indifferent to the outcome of the battle between good and evil.* That would make him a God who sits on the moral fence of the world and says, "I don't care what happens to them. Let them sin if they want to, that's their business. I'm not going to interfere in their lives." So whenever the biblical picture of a holy God who gets angry about sin seems old-fashioned and frightening, try to imagine something a whole lot scarier—*an apathetic God who doesn't care.* Imagine what it would be like to live in a world like ours if God were personally indifferent and morally neutral. That would be a terrifying nightmare.

It is the reality of a holy God who is irreconcilably opposed to all sin that makes life tolerable in a world like ours. For this means that God cares enough to get angry when we sin, because He cares enough to want the very best for us. It means too that we know which side God is on—He has declared Himself on the side of right and righteousness. That's comforting—not scary! And it can keep us from trying to bridge the great gap between us and God by trying to change His holy nature.

The Freudian Way

We are using the name of Sigmund Freud merely as representative. He is usually considered the father of psychoanalysis, and of all psychological schools of thought which attempt to bridge the chasm by trying to change the nature of sin. This philosophy either denies there is a chasm by lowering God's standards for us, or narrows the chasm to a mere gully which is easy to jump over.

Someone has contrasted Jesus and Freud in this way. Christ says to sinners, "Go and sin no more." Freud says to them, "Go and mourn no sin." While this is obviously oversimplified, it does highlight the basic error of all who would explain the gap of guilt *merely as a matter of guilt feelings.*

Our feelings of guilt from so-called sins and failures, they say, are the result of various taboos and rules placed on our consciences by cultural and social influences. Parents, teachers, religions, the laws of our societies are among the authority sources which help form our ideas of right and wrong. They create our value systems and thus our feelings of guilt or approval. The way to get rid of those feelings is to realize that the rules come from human opinions and are quite relative. We all have different standards and these are constantly changing. There are no absolutes, they claim, no really fixed standards; since we establish them, we can also change them and thus bridge the chasm.

We see the tragic results of this philosophy in the sexual

revolution of our times. Perhaps the most extreme present-day example is the change in attitude toward homosexual behavior on the part of many secular psychologists. What was once looked upon as *a sin to be avoided or a sickness to be treated* has come to be regarded as *a lifestyle to be accepted,* perhaps even *a gift to be celebrated.* The amazing fact is that this has taken place within a matter of a few years and has even affected, or should we say infected, some Christian circles. This is all the more amazing when you realize that every reference to homosexuality in Scripture is negative. It is a classic example of totally erasing the gap by eliminating the standard. It is also typical of what happens when the moral principles of God's Word are no longer considered the basis of right and wrong.

It is true that times and traditions do fashion some of the cultural norms of our conscience. There are many examples of this in the Bible itself. But the universal standards do not change. They are written into humankind.

What may be known about God is plain . . . because God made it plain to them. For since the creation of the world God's invisible qualities—His eternal power and divine nature—have been clearly seen, being understood from what has been made, *so that men are without excuse* . . . the requirements of the law are written on their hearts, their consciences also bearing witness (Romans 1:19-20; 2:15, italics added).

The Bible teaches a general revelation of some universal standards with corresponding ideas of guilt and atonement. Studies by anthropologists confirm that there seems to be a universal intuition about the gap between sinful humans and God. What various peoples do to bridge the gap varies widely, and may be very wrong. But the basic *intuition behind the acts is very right.* In one way or another they all seem to be saying, "Without the shedding of blood [suffering] there is no forgiveness" (Hebrews 9:22).

I saw the attempt at self-atonement in India, as I would watch a Hindu woman use her body as a living yardstick to measure out her length for the five-mile journey to the local temple; or watch chanting Shiite Muslim men strike their bare chests with their open hands until the blood came. I have also seen it in troubled Christians who come for counseling. Some self-destruct in a respectable way through overwork; some try to atone for their sins by the penance of inner self-depreciation; the emotionally disturbed ones use unusual and obsessive means of self-immolation. I am always amazed at this built-in sense of guilt and self-atonement. People may try to repress or ignore it, but it has interesting ways of revealing itself.

Dottie was a single young adult who came for counsel. She wasn't the least bit hesitant about sharing herself openly. I was struck by what seemed to be an almost compulsive need to reveal the garbage of her life in lurid detail. She was one of those modern, "liberated" Christians who feel sorry for pastors, thinking we live in a sheltered and antiseptic world. They go out of their way to tell us about the real world. A part of their mission is to enlighten us poor deprived souls of the joys of their new freedom.

Dottie would pause occasionally in her x-rated recital, look at me as if I were Exhibit A of life before the Enlightenment, and say with a confident smile, "Now I don't want you to get any idea that I feel guilty about this."

I must admit to a perversity which leads me to play the game with this type, and so I would say, "Oh no, of course not. I understand—no guilt."

Then I began to observe some body language from Dottie, as she kept taking sheets of Kleenex from the box I always keep on a side table. Not to wipe away tears— naturally not—since she felt no guilt; but one by one, shredding the tissues into little pieces. The pile on the table grew higher and higher. What fascinated me most was that she was completely unaware of the shredding ritual. After awhile, I decided to abandon my indirect counseling role. So I interrupted the latest chapter of her true confessions and said rather abruptly, "Excuse me, Dottie, but I don't believe what you're telling me."

"What do you mean? It's the truth, honestly."

"I believe your stories, but I don't believe your big story."

"My big story?"

"I don't believe your story about not feeling guilty about all this garbage in your life. In fact, I have the feeling your pile of guilt is as high as the mountain of Kleenex you've made on the table there."

She looked down in shocked disbelief. Obviously embarrassed, she sat silently staring at the shredded tissues. I was silent, but the Holy Spirit, whom Jesus promised would "convict the world of guilt in regard to sin," spoke loud and clear. Slowly Dottie reached for another Kleenex, and this time made proper use of it. "You're right," she sniffled. "I think I was hoping I'd not feel guilty if I was just honest about my sins. But down deep I knew better, and I knew that you knew better. I guess I was really hoping you wouldn't let me get by with it." We read together the Phillips' translation of that wonderful passage in Colossians 2:13-15 where Paul describes Christ's work on the cross.

> He has forgiven you all your sins: Christ has utterly wiped out the damning evidence of broken laws and commandments which always hung over our heads, and has completely annulled it by nailing it over His own head on the cross. And then, having drawn the sting of all the powers ranged against us, He exposed them, shattered, empty and defeated, in His final

glorious triumphant act!

Dottie came to understand that she didn't need to tear up either her sins or her Kleenex, or do any other unconscious acts of penance. Christ had shredded all her sin on the cross and set her free from their guilt, if she would but confess them to Him and trust what He had done for her. She discovered we can't bridge the gap by denying it exists, but only by trusting the One who bridged it as He "bore our sins in His body on the tree" (1 Peter 2:24). What a joy it was in future sessions to work with the Spirit in helping Dottie clean up her act and live as a daughter of God.

The Pharisaical Way

There is yet another unsuccessful method of trying to bridge the chasm, one often used by more legalistic Christians. Theirs is the way of obedience to a precise and codified set of rules. They use God's commandments as the main materials of the bridge. Man-made do's and don'ts are the nuts, bolts, and rivets to hold the main beams together. Very carefully they construct what appears to be a strong bridge, with their tightly knit scheme of externalized laws, rules, and regulations. The Owner's Manual which accompanies it covers every detail of the bridge. Then they swing that prefabricated bridge over the chasm and carefully, prayerfully, weld it into place. It seems to fit perfectly. Its intricate design, massive size, and inflexible quality give the appearance of immense strength. And as they walk across, they believe they have bridged the gap, and even enjoy a temporary sense of peace and security.

Prior to the coming of grace into his life, Paul constructed such a bridge. He tells about it in his Philippian letter (3:5-6), "a Hebrew of the Hebrews; in regard to the law, a Pharisee . . . as for legalistic righteousness, fault-less." And, of course, it was chiefly the Pharisees of Jesus' day who had constructed such a scheme. With their 612 detailed regulations for daily living, they had honed righteousness to an exact science. The only problem was that as they kept all those rules, they missed the heart of the matter—the law of love. The fiercest display of Jesus' white-hot anger was for the Pharisees, on a day when they were more interested in keeping laws than in Jesus' healing a man with a shriveled hand (Mark 3:1-5).

Many a sincere Christian has tried to please God and bridge the gap this same way, only to discover that in God's sight it is the most displeasing way of all. It never brings lasting peace because there's always one more rule that some person or group adds to the list. Also its followers are never quite sure they really kept the law the way they should have. This is an unsafe bridge which will one day collapse in a storm.

That's what happened many years ago to a very famous bridge. Finished early in 1940, the Tacoma Narrows Bridge in Washington State was a masterpiece of engineering. A 2,800-foot suspension bridge, it provided a much-needed crossing over the waters of the Puget Sound. It cost $75 million, a staggering expenditure at the time. It attracted so much attention that a local insurance company used it as an advertising slogan. Ads reading, "As Safe As the Tacoma Bridge," helped its insurance business flourish—but only for a few months. On November 7, 1940, a high wind began blowing in the Sound, and no one knows exactly what happened next. One conjecture was that because of the unusual terrain, wind trapped in that location would actually have the effect of doubling in velocity. So the 42-mile-an-hour wind of that afternoon had the effect of 84-miles-an-hour.

Whatever the cause, the bridge began to sway slightly. That was nothing new—the media had already affectionately named the bridge "Gallopin' Gertie." But this time the swaying got steadily worse until the bridge was in a violent front-and-back oscillation like a walking caterpillar. Several terrifying incidents of high drama took place as drivers climbed out of their vehicles and crawled back on the highway bridge which was now like a washboard. Within minutes the gigantic structure splintered into pieces and crashed into the Sound. Fortunately, the only loss of life was one animal. The embarrassed insurance company had to hire anyone they could find, at ridiculously high wages, to go all over the Northwest to take down their ad—"As Safe As the Tacoma Bridge." When the bridge was finally rebuilt in 1951, the engineers gave special attention to remedy what they felt might have been the original defect, "insufficient torsional and vertical stiffness in the main girders which were only eight feet deep."[1]

Jesus ended His Sermon on the Mount with a brief parable. It was not about a bridge but it did concern construction problems. The failure of the one house resulted because its foundation had not been dug sufficiently deep into the rock. So when "the storms rose, and the winds blew and beat against that house . . . it fell with a great crash" (Matthew 7:24-27).

The Bible makes clear that any attempt to bridge the chasm by trying to keep the law, however perfectly, is doomed. The very purpose of the law is *to widen the chasm, not reduce it.*

> Now we know that whatever the law says, it says to those who are under the law, so that every mouth may be silenced and the whole world held accountable to God. Therefore no one will be declared righteous in His sight by observing the law; rather, through the law we become conscious of sin (Romans 3:19-20).

The Avis Way

"We'll try harder." This motto is at the heart of the performance-minded, and describes millions of Christians, yes, genuinely reborn children of God who live daily lives of quiet desperation. Going through a seemingly endless cycle of failure, guilt, repentance, confession, forgiveness, restoration, trying something new only to be followed by another failure, more guilt, another repentance, confession, forgiveness, restoration—and so on, *ad infinitum.* Or perhaps we should say, *ad nauseum,* since they get sick and tired of the effort and a kind of spiritual disillusionment creeps over them.

This can lead to several possible serious results, one being the sheer physical and emotional exhaustion which comes from trying harder to do better. Some people living in this overloaded stress situation, crack up, and experience what is commonly called a nervous breakdown.

Others, tired of the losing battle, settle into a twilight zone of defeat and depression, ever looking for some new spiritual high which always seems to elude them. Some become angry at what appears to be their unappeasable conscience and an unpleasable God and throw faith overboard. Though it may not seem to be so on the surface, this spiritual breakaway is really worse than an emotional breakdown.

Yet others, blessed with a strong constitution and stubborn determination, hang in there, but live with various combinations of emotional and spiritual problems. They are the performance-trapped Christians of this book.

What is the basic fallacy in the Avis way? Why doesn't it ever work? *Because you can't jump across a chasm in two leaps!* You only get one chance! When God's Word says we have "all sinned and fallen short," that's exactly what it means—fallen short. If you don't make it in one leap, you miss the other side. And it doesn't make any difference whether you missed it by one foot or one hundred yards—or one inch, for that matter. When you fall short of the other side, you fall right down into the canyon.

On September 8, 1974, stunt man Evel Knievel attempted to vault Idaho's Snake River Canyon. Prior to this Knievel had achieved notoriety with his stunt riding on motorcycles. He would take off from a wooden ramp and at very high speeds sail across snarls of live rattlesnakes or lines of parked cars. He was seriously injured several times and boasted he had broken every major bone in his body except his neck. This attempt to rocket across a fearsome chasm was his most daring feat.

On that day he flashed a check for $6 million, purportedly his advance fee from the anticipated 200,000 spectators and the closed-circuit TV receipts. Actually only a few motorcycle gangs and about 15,000 people gathered at Twin Falls to watch him soar across the canyon. But his Sky Cycle never made it. Fortunately for him, the landing parachute enabled it to drift down to the river's edge. Rescue helicopters brought him back up, bruised and humiliated but not seriously injured. The 1975 *Encyclopedia Britannica Yearbook* aptly described it as "the year's most spectacular failure!"

Actually, it is a vivid illustration of humankind's most common failure—a prideful and evil attempt to cross the moral chasm and "become as God." It is doomed to failure, for Scripture assures us there's no way to make it. Because we are fallen beings, we lack the power and will always fall short. And no matter how hard or how many times we try we will always come up short and fall again. It is indeed a vicious cycle and there's no way to break out of it in our own strength.

Thank God there is a better way—His way. God's gracious provision for bridging the canyon, the way of grace, is the only answer. I can hardly wait to tell you about it.

But first we need to look at an extreme type of performance-based Christianity. It is commonly called *perfec-*

tionism, or neurotic perfectionism. This is the most serious form of the disease. Let's see where the seeds of this sickness are sown, how it incubates and develops and some of the false cures which are proposed—solutions which do not bring answers but only become parts of the problem itself.

Six.

THE CONSEQUENCES
OF DYSGRACE

Jesus comes with all His grace,
Comes to save a fallen race;
Object of our glorious hope,
Jesus comes to lift us up.

He hath our salvation wrought,
He our captive souls hath bought,
He hath reconciled to God,
He hath washed us in His blood.

We are now His lawful right,
Walk as children of the light;
We shall soon obtain the grace,
Pure in heart to see His face.

I believe that God intended parental grace to be the chief means of counteracting the Fall. However, this does *not* mean that even the best possible Christian parenting can *do away with* the Fall. The finest home cannot make a child's nature morally neutral or spiritually good, nor can it guarantee that the child will automatically choose the right. Christian parents who overload themselves with guilt need to remember something—Adam and Eve were the only people who ever had *perfect parenting* and yet they chose the wrong! We are still fallen sinners both by *nature* and by *choice,* and thus stand in need of God's saving grace. Parental grace cannot remove the *consequences* of the Fall, but it can provide the greatest *counteraction* to it. For it communicates agape love and undeserved grace in concrete and understandable terms. In fact, it operates by the same principles God used in the Incarnation. "The Word became flesh and lived for a while among us. We have *seen* His glory . . . full of grace and truth" (John 1:14). "That which was from the beginning, which we have *heard,* which we have *seen* with our *eyes,* which we have *looked at* and our *hands have touched* . . . the life *appeared; we have seen it* . . . we proclaim to you what we've *seen and heard* . . ." (1 John 1:1-3). The words I have italicized all refer to physical senses—seeing, hearing, touching. They point to concrete experiences, not abstract concepts.

A mother was trying to reassure her little girl as she put her to bed in a darkened room. "Honey, you don't need to be scared. Remember God is going to be right here with you." The little girl replied, "I know, Mama, but I need a God with skin on Him." Children don't think in abstract concepts but in concrete pictures. When my grandson heard us talk about letting Jesus live in our hearts, he looked puzzled. "But how does He get into my heart? Does He come through my belly button?" A young child's world is very physical, very literal. Ideas and mental concepts will come later. For them, words need to become flesh and blood, skin and bodies, faces and eyes which smile, feet that walk, hands that touch, arms that hug. The strongest influences on them come through real live human relationships with people they consider important, with their "significant others."

Parents are the most effective communicators of truths, values, concepts, and lifestyles, because they *incarnate them in concrete relationships.* This is the reason we have said children learn a language of relationships long before they learn to speak a single word. And this is why parental grace is so incredibly important. Through it we get our earliest experience of genuine—though imperfect—agape love. Through it we can grow up experiencing a *quality* of grace similar to what we receive from God Himself. This taste of love and grace, though partial, whets our appetite for God's perfect love and grace. More than any other single factor, it is intended to prepare us for the advent of God's saving grace in our lives. It does not guarantee our salvation, for we can still refuse to respond to God or to receive His gift. Its central purpose is to pave the way for receiving God's grace.

That's exactly why parental dysgrace is so terribly destructive. Because grace has the highest potential for *helping*, dysgrace has the highest potential for *hindering*. The greatest means of dispensing prevenient and preparatory grace can turn into the greatest means of distorting it.

The Seeds of Perfectionism

Let us now combine several important truths of Scripture with those of developmental psychology. This will help us understand some of the reasons why we become who we are. In this process we shall discover the main causes and consequences of the most extreme and painful form of performance-based living we generally call *perfectionism*.

THE ORIGINS AND GROWTH OF A PERFECTIONIST

THE TRUE AND UNIQUE SELF
(OUR POTENTIAL SELFHOOD IN CHRIST)
With inborn needs to be met for its proper development through
PARENTAL GRACE

Listed in Luke 2:51-52. Physical, Mental, Emotional, Social, Spiritual and Relational. Nourishment and Nurture, Discipline and Instruction.

BUT THESE NEEDS ARE NOT MET—PARENTAL DYSGRACE

INDIRECTLY	DIRECTLY
By deprivation of physical nourishment, emotional nurture, security, unconditional acceptance, belongingness, affection, affirmation, discipline, and instruction.	By rejection, withdrawal, ridicule, injustice, mixed messages (double binds), excessive legalism, cruelty, overcoercion, abuse (verbal, emotional, physical, or sexual).

A FALSE SUPERSELF DEVELOPS
An idealized image, a fantasy and false picture of self is developed in the attempt to get these needs filled, and thus be pleasing, accepted, loved, and to be unique.

TO BE THIS IDEALIZED SELF NOW BECOMES THE CHIEF GOAL.
IT CONSUMES ALL EMOTIONAL AND SPIRITUAL ENERGIES.
IT IS THE SEARCH FOR GLORY.

This self gradually moves from "I'm UNIQUE," to "I'm SPECIAL" to "I'm BETTER." My NEEDS become CLAIMS UPON OTHERS—"I'm ENTITLED TO."

THE CHIEF CHARACTERISTICS OF THE SUPERSELF ARE

NEED TO BE PERFECT	DISTORTED PRIORITIES	NECESSITY OF A SCAPEGOAT	ANGRY NEED TO PROVE

THE TYRANNY OF THE OUGHTS

I OUGHT to be able to be Superself but I CANNOT. This failure to
reach unrealistic, unattainable (godlike) expectations results in
frustration, depression, and anger (rage) against a sense of
unfairness and injustice. This results in

| HURTS | HUMILIATIONS | FEARS | ANGER |

AND

LOW SELF-IMAGE

| SELF-BELITTLEMENT
SELF-ACCUSATIONS | SELF-BLAME
SELF-ATONEMENT | SELF-TORTURE
SELF-DESTRUCTION |

FALSE PERFECTIONISTIC SOLUTIONS
AND POSSIBLE PERSONALITY PATTERNS

MASTERY	SELF-EFFACEMENT	RESIGNATION
Excessive Need For **Self-Esteem.** (Moving **against** people) Need for power, personal achievement, admiration, prestige, and recognition. Need to feel superior.	Excessive Need to **Belong.** (Moving **toward** people) Weak, helpless, over-dependent, compliant, submissive, and loving. Need for approval, fear of disapproval.	Excessive Need for **Control.** (Moving **away from** people) Detached, resigned, over-independent, self-sufficient, unassailable, need to feel invulnerable.

(FIGURE 1)

91

We shall also look at some of the false ways in which people try to solve the problem.

I freely admit my indebtedness to certain scholars and writers who are generally classified as social psychologists.[1] I believe their insights come closest to those of the Bible with its central emphasis on personal relationships within family and community.

The older I grow and the more I counsel, the more I am amazed by the unfathomable mystery of human personality. There is *only One*, our Lord Himself, who "knew all men. He did not need man's testimony about man, for He knew what was in a man" (John 2:24-25). He alone who is *the Truth* knows *the truth* about the human personality. The best we can offer is *truths about the truth*. To offer more than that is to lessen the mystery and weaken our responsibility. *When we do this we take away from the fact that ultimately we are responsible before God for the choices which make us who and what we are.* It's helpful to try to explain, but we must never explain so well that *we explain away*.

Take a careful look at the chart, The Origin and Growth of a Perfectionist, scanning the whole process to get an overall picture. If you don't understand a particular section, leave it and continue to read. We are now going to break up the total figure into several parts, picture each one separately and explain it in detail.

There is a lot of confusion among Christians regarding the word *self*. That's because we use the word to convey several different meanings. Taken negatively, *self* can mean the sinful, carnal, person-centered ego, the "flesh" which Scripture indicates needs to be crucified.

I am using *self* in the positive sense of your basic personhood, the self God intended you to be—imperishable, indestructible, and of eternal value in His sight. It is your basic human personhood, the unique you with all the possibilities for your particular personality with its talents.

> ### THE TRUE AND UNIQUE SELF
> #### (OUR POTENTIAL SELFHOOD IN CHRIST)
> With inborn needs to be met for its proper development through
> ### PARENTAL GRACE
> Listed in Luke 2:51-52. Physical, Mental, Emotional, Social, Spiritual and Relational. Nourishment and Nurture, Discipline and Instruction.

The God of this universe, who can't even stand to make two snowflakes alike, has designed each of us to be uniquely ourselves.

Your selfhood is what makes you to be you. In God's plan it is this potential person who, through salvation and sanctification, is to become more and more transformed into the likeness of Christ (2 Corinthians 3:18). This self is made for both earthly and eternal fellowship with God and other people.

But this self doesn't suddenly emerge. You and I were born of human parents, and from them we inherited bodies, brains, and directives about many things which have been coded into our genes. Furthermore, we were born into families which created the environment and the atmosphere in which this self would grow and develop. God designed this in such a way that we all had a whole set of needs which had to be met if we were to become the unique persons He wants us to be. These run all the way from basic physical needs for food and protection to emotional needs for security and affection. In chapter 3, we saw our model for this in the section on "Parental Grace in Jesus' Life." Our deepest needs are for personal relationships with other humans and, above all, with God. If these needs are reasonably well met, our divinely designed selves will develop with the potential of becoming whole persons.

BUT THESE NEEDS ARE NOT MET—PARENTAL DYSGRACE

INDIRECTLY	DIRECTLY
By deprivation of physical nourishment, emotional nurture, security, unconditional acceptance, belongingness, affection, affirmation, discipline, and instruction.	By rejection, withdrawal, ridicule, injustice, mixed messages (double binds), excessive legalism, cruelty, overcoercion, abuse (verbal, emotional, physical, or sexual).

Let us take a closer look at some of these divinely implanted needs which must be met for healthy growth and development to occur. Besides receiving food and physical care, children need to feel they are accepted, loved, and affirmed. They need a predictable, reliable sense of security and belongingness. They are made for agape-love, which includes discipline (setting limits) as well as genuine affection. And most of all, *children need an atmosphere where they feel these needs are met because of who they are and not because of what they do.*

It is in the quality of the earliest interpersonal relationships that children have their first taste of grace, or its opposite, dysgrace. It is here the good seeds of undeserved, unconditional acceptance, or the deadly seeds of conditional, performance-based acceptance are sown. Often in these early years deep-seated impressions about life are implanted which will have long-lasting effects on the way their personalities develop.

In certain kinds of homes, these needs are not met. The more obvious ones are homes where alcoholism or drug addiction make life extremely unpredictable and where children end up having to meet the needs of their parents. Or homes where physical, emotional, and verbal cruelty are common. Certainly all forms of sexual abuse (heterosexual and homosexual) are terribly damaging, since sexuality and personal identity so often develop together.

A college student shared with me that since he was a child he had been attacked by his mother. Whenever she lost her temper, she would grab him by the arm, pull him to his feet, and throw him against the wall. Once this caused a dislocation of his shoulder and he was forced to tell the doctor he had fallen from a tree. Another student tremblingly described to me the way her older brothers sexually violated her. As they took turns, the others would watch and make fun of her. Since this usually happened when both parents were away at work, she felt a lot of bitterness regarding their failure to protect her from the abuse or from the threats which silenced her. Saddest of all are those children from homes where these situations exist side by side with participation in church life and a professed commitment to biblical Christianity.

But there is also the less obvious deprivation where the growing child is robbed of emotional and spiritual nurture in more subtle ways, perhaps from a parent who outwardly goes through all the motions of caring but inwardly rejects the child. How often I have heard statements like, "My folks gave me everything I wanted—toys, clothes, money—but they never gave me love and affection. I'd trade all of that to know they really wanted me." The key factor in children feeling rejected is the emotional knowledge that they were not loved and wanted for who they were. This can take the form of long-term neglect, disinterest, or lack of discipline because parents don't care enough. Or it can come from a completely different angle. I have heard it often from children of missionaries and preachers, "I never felt that I mattered, or that they cared about me for who I was as a person. The only thing about me they were really interested in was how I would affect their spiritual reputation."

Some parents withdraw affection as a means of punishment, or employ guilt as a means of control. One lady said, "My mother was the travel agent for my guilt trips—

mostly one way." Perhaps the most subtle form of conditional love is the use of mixed messages and double binds. One of Jesus' most psychologically profound statements is, "Simply let your 'Yes' be 'Yes' and your 'No,' 'No' " (Matthew 5:37). Parents who are constantly saying "Yes" and "No" at the same time create deep confusion and contradictory emotions in their children. For example, when a child asks, "Mama, may I go out and play?" the parent should not answer with a confusing, "Well, yes, go ahead, but remember I'll be here cleaning your room." It is much healthier to say, "Yes, after you clean your room (or do your homework)," or "No, I need your help today."

Do you remember some of the classic humorous double binds? You give your son two T-shirts for Christmas. When he wears one, you say to him in an injured tone, "Oh, so you didn't like the other one, eh?" Or, "I love you—even though you're stupid—or fat—or ugly—or clumsy—or even though you are a girl." Mixed messages put children in the impossible no-win position of "damned if you do and damned if you don't." This leads them to feel that nothing they can possibly do will please their parents, that there's no way to win their approval and affection.

Another area where many sincere Christian parents don't realize how much they promote an atmosphere of conditional, performance-earned acceptance is by excessive emphasis on the do's and don'ts of the Christian life. Certainly, it is the responsibility of parents to teach their children the scriptural commandments of God. They must do this both by precept—*what* they teach—and example—*how* they live. But most crucial is *the spirit in which this is done.* In Ephesians 6:4 and Colossians 3:21, Paul cautions parents not to "exasperate" or "embitter" children. Other translations expand the meaning. "Do not provoke your children to anger . . . lest they become discouraged." "Don't overcorrect . . . lest they grow up feeling inferior and frustrated."

There is an important principle involved here that we can put into a formula: R + R - R = R + R. *Rules and Regulations minus Relationships equals Resentment and Rebellion.* Rules and regulations and their enforcement by discipline must be put in the context of loving, grace-full relationships, or they will result in frustration and resentment. It is perfectly necessary and proper to enforce Christian standards and family rules by correcting and disciplining our children. But we must make it plain to them that our actions are because of *what they have done, and not because of who they are.* It's one thing to say, "We're doing this because we love you too much to let you grow up doing that." It's quite another thing to say, "You are a naughty boy," or "You are a bad girl," or "You always do things like that," or "Do you want to grow up to be like _____?" or "I don't know why we ever had you in the first place." The first is *to correct wrong behavior, to assure them that though they have broken a commandment, their relationship with you is intact.* The second is *to demean and put them down as persons and infer not only your disapproval but also your nonacceptance.* That is why legalistic and grace-less Christian homes can be emotionally destructive, even though on the surface everyone *seems to be doing the right things.*

It is not as if a child consciously decides to become a different person. The decision happens deep in the personality, below the level of awareness. If we could put it into words, it would sound something like this, "Obviously I am not accepted or loved as I am. Nothing I can do seems pleasing to them. So I'd better become something else—someone else. Maybe then I'll be acceptable and lovable."

And slowly but surely, an idealized fantasy self emerges, a superself which can live up to all the expectations and demands of the parents. If this begins when the child is

---

A FALSE SUPERSELF DEVELOPS

An idealized image, a fantasy and false picture of self is developed
in the attempt to get these needs filled, and thus be pleasing,
accepted, loved, and to be unique.

TO BE THIS IDEALIZED SELF NOW BECOMES THE CHIEF GOAL.
IT CONSUMES ALL EMOTIONAL AND SPIRITUAL ENERGIES.
IT IS THE SEARCH FOR GLORY.

This self gradually moves from "I'm UNIQUE," to "I'm SPECIAL" to "I'm
BETTER." My NEEDS become CLAIMS UPON OTHERS—"I'm ENTITLED TO."

---

very young, after a while what the true self really thinks,
feels, or desires is ignored, since physical, emotional, and
spiritual energies are going into attaining and maintaining
the superself.

All of us are afraid for others to know who we really
are. This fear began when Adam and Eve hid from God
behind the trees of the Garden, and from one another by
a covering of fig leaves (Genesis 3:7-8). This innate fear
of revealing our real selves can intertwine with the need
to become false selves. Sin is thus greatly compounded by
the damaged emotions resulting from dysgrace as the pursuit of a false selfhood is an all-consuming passion. It
becomes what Karen Horney so fittingly calls "the search
for glory."[2]

In this process, the God-given feeling of *"I'm unique"* is
twisted into *"I'm special,"* and then into *"I'm better than."*
When the superself grows up, it becomes *"I'm entitled to."*
Needs have been turned into *claims*—claims upon God
and others. "Since I'm so special, I'm entitled to special
treatment." When that special consideration is not forth-
coming, the person may become angry with others and
God.

In such a process, the real self is either denied or de-
spised, and has no chance to develop. This is why such
persons later will often say, "I don't really know who I
am—and am afraid to find out." They sense an inner

emptiness, phoniness, and a deep feeling of loneliness, and nothing seems to fill the void. Whatever they try is blocked by the superself and never reaches the real self. The creation of an unreal and false self is often the price of emotional survival, for there is no other way to bear the mental pain of rejection. But alienation from the true self is a terrible price to pay, and a tragic waste of personhood divinely designed "before the creation of the world" (Ephesians 1:4, 11).

This is the reason why so many Christians play a comparison game and never feel like they "measure up." Instead of allowing their God-ordained self to "grow up in every way into Christ" (Ephesians 4:15), they keep trying to be super Christians, who need to be *better than* other people. The trouble with this is that they can always find another person who is still better and so the striving to be the greatest continues.

Some day this false self needs to die so that the true self may be allowed to live and to grow as it once did. In this sense, a spiritual rebirth, death, and resurrection must take place.

THE CHIEF CHARACTERISTICS OF THE SUPERSELF ARE			
NEED TO BE PERFECT	DISTORTED PRIORITIES	NECESSITY OF A SCAPEGOAT	ANGRY NEED TO PROVE

We come now to the four major characteristics of the superself.

• The need to be perfect. The superself is a super person who must do things perfectly. Or, at least, *ought* to be able to. The feeling is, "If I can just do and be what *they* want, *they* will accept, love, and appreciate me." The tragedy is that *they* are often persons who are never satisfied or who don't really know what they want. The superself tries harder and harder to please. The performance treadmill is now in operation with "if only" as its watchword. Such futile trying produces a deep despair in the personality that may not surface for many years.

That's the way it was with Margaret, a woman in her thirties. In spite of her dedication to Christ and a consistent devotional life, her marriage and family were being affected by her outbursts of anger and serious bouts with depression. It didn't take long to discover that she had internalized the voice of an unpleasant, perfectionistic mother until she thought it was the voice of conscience and God. Now she was her own harshest taskmaster, demanding perfection of herself, even as others had demanded it of her. Hurt, anger, and guilt kept the treadmill going. Margaret needed to face the hurts and then forgive those who had hurt her.

During one of our prayer times for the healing of some painful memories, a scene emerged which she had not shared with me. She said she had not wanted to look at it, but while we were praying, God gave her the courage to face the pain. She was just a youngster practicing for her first piano recital. She wanted to play her piece perfectly, and so she worked and worked, until the piece was memorized. At the recital, she played it perfectly. As she walked off the stage, her piano teacher grasped her elbow and said softly, "Excellent, Margaret, you played it perfectly!" She was so excited. But when she took her place beside her mother, there was a pause and then this whisper in her ear, "Your slip was showing the whole time." Margaret sobbed as she told God about this, and about many other scars. Best of all, she received grace to forgive, and also to be forgiven for the resentments she had carried for years. It was the crisis beginning to a process of changing from living under the law to living under grace.

● The need for a scapegoat. Not even the superself can be perfect. If we *have to see ourselves as perfect*, there is only one solution—we must have someone to blame it on.

We "could have, should have, would have . . . *if only.*" If only Mother hadn't done this. . . . If only Dad had done that. . . . If only brother/sister were different. . . . If only that teacher had or hadn't. . . . If only our preacher/ church would. . . . If only God had/hadn't/would. . . . If only my husband/wife/children. . . . The list is endless.

The only way superself can maintain the myth of being super is to put the responsibility for failure on somebody or something else. Even people who *seem* to put all the blame *on themselves* inwardly believe the real fault lies with those who caused them to be what they are.

This is one of the chief reasons why performance-minded and perfectionistic people are so hard to live with. Whatever happens, *blame must be placed somewhere.* This need is destructive to relationships.

• The angry need to prove oneself. I have yet to counsel a perfectionist who isn't deeply angry inside. With some people, when the anger is tapped into, it comes gushing out like an oil well. Until they experience grace at that level, the superself will remain angry, vindictive, and have to prove itself. Forgiveness is crucially important in the healing of this disease. Forgiveness—given to others and ourselves, and received from God—defuses the resentment and helps us deal with the need to prove ourselves acceptable and loved.

• The distortion of priorities and values. The superself must prove itself superior, and engages in a relentless search for an area to do so. This is where the twisted values of our sinful culture exert such pressure. The terrible overemphasis on athletics, grades, physical beauty, thinness, sexual attractiveness, fun, success (including false ideas of spiritual success), material wealth, things, clothes, cars—the list is endless—all can become the wrong centers around which the superself revolves.

Or, the superself can invert the list and then *feel superior because it doesn't seek any of these things.* The superself may do all it can to *not achieve*. It may seek the *weird and the unusual, and major on being different.*

I have stopped being surprised at *any false value, any misplaced, displaced, distorted priority which people use to show that they're different, special, and super.* When we refuse to accept and develop our real selves in their God-designed uniqueness, we pay the consequences of fashioning and developing false selves which are sometimes off the wall! Many such perfectionists cling *with incredible tenacity* to these places where they feel *different and superior.* They often tell me, "But if I gave that up I'd be ordinary, just like everyone else." I often reply, "Welcome. Join the human race!"

THE TYRANNY OF THE OUGHTS

I OUGHT to be able to be Superself but I CANNOT. This failure to reach unrealistic, unattainable (godlike) expectations results in frustration, depression, and anger (rage) against a sense of unfairness and injustice. This results in

In striving to be special, the superself receives extremely strong motivation from a driving sense of "oughtness." We *ought* to be this kind of self, but we can't quite make it. Why? Because we keep putting unreachable goals and unattainable standards before ourselves. And strangely enough, if we get near them, we will raise them even higher. Imagine a high-jumper in the Olympics. Every time they raise the bar, he clears it. Finally he jumps higher than all the rest and wins. But instead of standing on the center platform and receiving the prized gold medal, he raises the bar even higher. He tries several times, and falls with each attempt. Then he walks away dejected, feeling as if he lost the contest. Many perfectionists live this way. This sense of failure naturally produces frustration and anger against other people and often against God. As long as they live under the bondage of the performance-treadmill, they will be angry. Life will seem unfair and God will seem unjust. This will result in a range of negative feelings.

HURTS   HUMILIATIONS   FEARS   ANGER

AND

LOW SELF-IMAGE

SELF-BELITTLEMENT   SELF-BLAME   SELF-TORTURE
SELF-ACCUSATIONS   SELF-ATONEMENT   SELF-DESTRUCTION

The hurts and humiliations perfectionists suffer keep their anxieties and anger churning. And not all of the anger is directed outward, for perfectionists live with a unique *combination of pride and low self-esteem.* They *always* suffer from a self-depreciation that *comes from fearful pride.* They are afraid others will discover the terrible gap between their *real selves* and their *fantasy selves* and then reject them. So they beat the public to the punch. *They reject themselves by putting themselves down before anyone else can. In this way their false pride in their superself is kept intact.*

We see this prideful self-rejection every day in perfectionistic Christians who cannot accept compliments without going out of their way to belittle their accomplishments. They must impress you with their humility and not let you catch them with their pride showing!

You can see that low self-image increases in intensity and becomes much more serious as you read from left to right. It varies from the more normal put-downs on the left to forms of self-atonement in the center—the kind A.W. Tozer described as "the penance of perpetual regret." On the right, you reach the pathological level where people inflict hurt or pain on themselves, such as picking at, or cutting the skin, or pulling out their hair.

Self-despising becomes much more pathological in the

various forms of slow self-destruction—alcohol, drugs, excessive smoking, serious eating disorders like extreme overeating, anorexia, or bulemia. The ultimate is, of course, the quick self-destruction of suicide. Every reliable book on teenage suicide includes a warning about adolescents who think they have to be perfect and can't stand to live if they aren't. We have all witnessed the tragic results of this degree of self-hate, even in the lives of some who are sincerely trying to be good Christians.

In conclusion, we look at Karen Horney's classification of three *wrong solutions* to the dilemma of the perfectionist performance trap, and the possible personality patterns which can develop from them.[3] As we briefly describe them, keep in mind they are lifestyles—all-inclusive patterns of coping with life and relating to people. While they seem different from each other, they are all basically performance-based systems of living "under the law" rather than "under grace." They do not exclude one another. Persons can have some traits from more than one personality structure, but usually one type will be dominant over the others. They represent highly exaggerated and wrong ways of trying to meet the unfulfilled needs of our true selves.

- Mastery describes persons who feel an excessive need

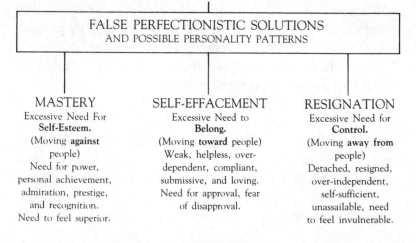

FALSE PERFECTIONISTIC SOLUTIONS
AND POSSIBLE PERSONALITY PATTERNS

MASTERY	SELF-EFFACEMENT	RESIGNATION
Excessive Need For **Self-Esteem.**	Excessive Need to **Belong.**	Excessive Need for **Control.**
(Moving **against** people)	(Moving **toward** people)	(Moving **away from** people)
Need for power, personal achievement, admiration, prestige, and recognition. Need to feel superior.	Weak, helpless, over-dependent, compliant, submissive, and loving. Need for approval, fear of disapproval.	Detached, resigned, over-independent, self-sufficient, unassailable, need to feel invulnerable.

for recognition and admiration and try to win it by superior achievements in some area of life. They have to be not only good, but the best. This gives them a sense of power and domination over other people. They may indeed excel in their field of pursuit and tend to look down on those who don't. Their temptation is to reverse Christian values so they use people and love things. They exhibit qualities of hardness, craftiness, aggressive ambition, insensitivity to others' feelings, the ability to strike a hard bargain and to outmaneuver opponents. What they are saying is, "If I am strong and dominate people, they can't hurt me." It is very difficult for such damaged persons to accept love and grace and remove their masks of a false super-strong self.

• Self-effacement represents persons whose need for approval is so strong they will do anything to please people. They major in being submissive, compliant, and allowing others to make decisions. An all-absorbing "love" seems to them to be the answer to all their problems. They carry it to extremes so they never make waves or rock the boat. It's peace at any price. They rarely express an opinion or confront a person or a situation because they feel they really have nothing to contribute. This is a favorite stance for many Christians, who take this vice of excessive weakness and spiritualize it into a virtue by saying it is the way of Christian love. This is perhaps the greatest counterfeit of genuine love, which can be tough and confrontive when necessary. Self-effacing persons are really saying, "I will do anything if you'll just love me; for if you love me, then you won't hurt me."

Such persons often link up with their opposites to produce a sad and deadly combination which simply feeds one another's problems. Worst of all, it is often sanctified and blessed by some preachers and seminar leaders who misinterpret Ephesians 5:21-24 and promote this kind of destructive and neurotic relationship as if it were God's plan for marriage. It is often difficult for such Christians to receive grace, for they feel guilty and afraid and can't handle the freedom it brings.

• Resignation and detachment characterize those persons who want to be left alone. They feel if they don't get involved no one can hurt them. At any cost, they must move away from other people and not show any need for dependence. They require a lot of emotional space, and the intimate relationships of marriage may be so painful for them as to be intolerable. Many self-effacing persons who desperately need closeness and affection marry this kind of personality, because they appear to be the strong, silent type. It can become the sort of marriage where instead of complementing one another's needs, the partners drive each other into even greater extremes. It takes a lot of grace to save such a marriage, even when both partners are Christians.

In this chapter we have looked at the origin and development of the more extreme variety of performance-based Christians, perfectionists. We have also seen that any attempt to find freedom by our own efforts only leads us deeper into the mire. Let's turn now to the only solution and our only hope. God's greatest gift—grace.

Seven.

THE GOOD NEWS

Jesus! the name to sinners dear,
The name to sinners given;
It scatters all their guilty fear;
It turns their hell to heaven.

O that the world might taste and see,
The riches of His grace!
The arms of love that compass me
Would all mankind embrace.

For several chapters we have looked at the bad news—the moral chasm—and our utter inability to bridge it. Now let's take a look at the good news. Perhaps you've heard this good news–bad news story.

A farmer who had experienced several bad years went to see the manager of his bank.

"I've got some good news and some bad news to tell you. Which would you like to hear first?" he asked.

"Why don't you give me the bad news first and get it over with?" the banker replied.

"Okay. With the bad drought and inflation and all, I won't be able to pay anything on my mortgage this year; either on the principle or the interest."

"Well, that is pretty bad."

"It gets worse. I also won't be able to pay anything on the loan for all that machinery I bought, nor on the principle or interest."

"Wow, that is bad."

"It's worse than that. You remember I also borrowed to buy seeds and fertilizer and other supplies. Well, I can't pay anything on that either—principle or interest."

"That's awful—and that's enough! Tell me what the good news is."

"The good news," replied the farmer with a smile, "is that I intend to keep on doing business with you."

There's some rather profound theology in that story, provided we reverse the subjects. The good news of the Gospel is that in spite of our total moral bankruptcy, *God keeps on doing business with us.* Notwithstanding the hopelessness of our predicament, God has found a way to bridge the gap, restore us to a relationship with Himself, and to bring healing to the damaged areas of our personalities.

Paul exultantly exclaims, "Where sin abounded, grace did much more abound" (KJV). In the original Greek Paul uses the same root word for "abound" in both phrases. But the second time, in connection with grace, he adds the prefix *huper,* so that it literally means, "Where sin abounded, grace *superabounded.*" The Phillips version of this passage uses the imagery of the moral chasm to show that what was formerly totally impossible is now gloriously possible.

Though sin is shown to be wide and deep, thank God His grace is wider and deeper still! The whole outlook changes—sin used to be the master of men and in the end handed them over to death; now grace is the ruling factor, with righteousness its purpose and its end the bringing of men to the eternal life of God through Jesus Christ our Lord (Romans 5:20-21).

Paul is the great Apostle of Grace. Of the 155 New Testament references to grace, 133 belong to him. Grace opens his epistles, grace closes them, and grace is the keynote of everything in between. The word *grace* is the anglicized Latin word *gratia* which was used to translate the Greek word *charis* (pronounced karis). In ordinary Greek, *charis* meant gracefulness, graciousness, favor, or kindness. It could also mean the gracious response or gratitude of someone who had received a favor.

Paul puts *charis* into the context of the good news of the Christian Gospel to mean a freely bestowed favor. As he gives it several shades of meaning, *charis* truly becomes a many-splendored thing. Paul uses it especially to refer to what God has done for us in and through Jesus Christ. You could say grace is God's love in action on our behalf, freely giving us His forgiveness, His acceptance, and His favor. It is motivated only by God's love for us and not because of any worthiness or deservedness on our part. Grace is freely given, undeserved favor. In the Christian sense, it is essentially the redeeming activity of God in Christ. Not something done only in the past, it operates also in the present, and will continue throughout the future. This means that *grace and grace alone is, and always will be, the basis of our relationship with God.* "For by grace are you saved through faith; and that not of yourselves: it is the gift of God" (Ephesians 2:8, KJV). Those words are true for the vilest and most degraded sinner; they are equally true for the ripest and shiniest saint. *This grace base will never be replaced by something else.*

The Character of Grace
If grace is freely given, undeserved favor, then it is supremely important we understand some essential facts about it.

● Grace is undeserved. Grace has nothing to do with our merit or demerit, our sinfulness or worthiness. When the Bible says grace is free, it means that God is free to show His love and mercy toward us without the slightest limitation because of our sin. The moment you even bring up the question of unworthiness and undeservedness, you cancel out the idea of grace.

Jesus never once used the word *grace,* and of all the Gospel writers John alone used it to apply to Jesus (John 1:14, 16, 17). But as the saying goes, "Why waste words?" For the entire life of Christ was a nonstop demonstration of the fact that He offered the gift of salvation to everyone, *without any regard for their worthiness.* He was a living commentary upon His own words, "I have not come to call the righteous but sinners" (Matthew 9:13; Mark 2:17; Luke 5:32). Daily He incarnated grace—love, mercy, and salvation freely offered to people whose lives had no claim on it whatsoever. In fact, this is what always insulted "righteous" people—in His day, and ever since.

In the second century, a critic of Christianity named Celsus said the idea of God loving *sinners—bad people—*was "a thing unheard of in any other religion." He was absolutely right. That's what grace is about. That's what makes it different from other religions; they offer *good views* and *good advice*—"Be good, straighten up your life, clean up your act, get it together, live a good life and then, of course, you can come to God. Then you will be pleasing to God and He will love you." Only the Gospel of Christ is *good news*, the incredible message of grace. As A.W. Tozer put it, "Grace is the good pleasure of God that inclines Him to bestow benefit upon the undeserving."[1]

During the Napoleanic Wars, a young, battle-weary French soldier fell asleep while on guard duty. He was court-martialed, found guilty, and sentenced to death. His widowed mother somehow arranged an audience with the Emperor Napoleon himself. Falling prostrate at his feet she begged for her son's life to be spared, explaining he was her only child and her sole means of support. Napoleon grew weary of her pleas. "Madam, your son does not deserve mercy. He deserves to die," he said coldly. To which the mother immediately replied, "Of course, sire, you are right. That's why I am asking you to show mercy on him. If he were deserving, it wouldn't be mercy." Napoleon was so touched by the logic of her statement that he pardoned the soldier.

If we were deserving, it wouldn't be grace. It is undeserved and unmerited. It is God's free gift, completely unobstructed by our sin, our guilt, and our unworthiness.

● Grace is unearnable. Not only is grace undeserved, but it is also unearnable. Many of us start out on the highway of undeserved grace saying, "Of course, God accepts me just as I am. I know I am totally undeserving and have nothing to offer Him but my sins and failures. *But from this point on, He certainly expects me to live up to certain standards of performance.*" And then, like the Galatians, many of us who began in grace quite unintentionally decide that the continuation of God's gift of grace depends on how well we perform. We subtly assume we can earn or win God's approval and fill the performance gap by works. Not works in the former sense of good deeds or hard work or payments to charitable causes—we know better than that; but in the sense of taking the very channels of grace—prayer, Bible reading, witnessing, service—and turning them into Christian works of performance. We try to change the *grace base into a performance base*. But the grace base can never be replaced by anything else. This futile attempt by so many Christians is the source of their emotional and spiritual struggles.

After many years of pastoral ministry in which it has been my privilege to counsel people of varying races and cultures, I have come to a strong conclusion that the last thing we humans surrender to God is an admission of our helplessness to save ourselves. We will give up our sins, ambitions, money, name, fame, comfort—we are willing to sacrifice and surrender them all to God. But the most difficult, costly, and last thing we will give up is *our confidence that there is something we can do which will earn us a right relationship with God*. The second stanza of the hymn, "Rock of Ages," captures our inability so beautifully.

> Could my tears forever flow,
> Could my zeal no languor know,
> These for sin could not atone;
> Thou must save, and Thou alone.
> In my hands no price I bring;
> Simply to Thy cross I cling.

Until the truth conveyed in these lines becomes a living reality, we will not understand or experience the biblical meaning of grace. The writer of Hebrews reminds us that "without faith it is impossible to please Him" (11:6). This means that God is not pleased when we attempt to substitute righteousness by achievement through performance for salvation by grace through faith. He will not allow us to change the terms God has set for an acceptable, pleasing relationship with Himself. "It is by grace you have been saved, through faith—and this not from yourselves, it is the gift of God—not by works, so that no one can boast" (Ephesians 2:8-9). "Not from yourselves . . . so that no one can boast" means that God will not share His glory nor allow us to claim any of the credit for our salvation. Grace is a free gift. The moment we try to pay for it, it ceases to be grace for us.

• Grace is unrepayable. Some people try to turn the gift of grace into salvation by promissory note. This is similar to the attempt to earn grace, but places more emphasis on the future. "Lord, if You will forgive me and save me, I promise I will pay You back someday."

Some people try to make this repayment through *self-atonement*, by refusing to forgive themselves for past sins or failures; or not allowing themselves to enjoy the legitimate pleasures of life, such as sex within marriage, or a fun-filled vacation.

Others attempt repayment through *self-sacrifice*. This includes different forms of asceticism, like constantly giving up this or giving away that. Or adding this or that onto their lives as a way of self-discipline. I will always remember a student named Rodney who struggled to live in grace. He had an excellent head theology of grace, but kept derailing in his day-to-day life. Every time he came to see me, the list of activities and things he gave up for the Lord was longer. One day he arrived, sat down with a sigh of relief and said, "Well, I finally gave it up." "Gave up what, Rod?" I asked. "I took my whole stereo outfit and threw it in the garbage."

I must confess my mind wasn't totally on the counseling session at that moment. We had just come off the mission field and hadn't been able to afford a stereo as yet. My teenage kids kept putting it high on our list of American "necessities." When our session was over, I rushed out to where the college garbage was gathered, but I was too late. Someone had already retrieved Rod's expensive stereo! The next time I saw Rod he had still more to add to his ascetic list.

Some try to repay God through *service*. I've counseled missionaries who sadly admitted to me that repayment had been the real motivation for their sacrificial service. Their emphasis was on all they had "given up in order to serve the Lord." But in every case they had not found joy and fulfillment in their lives. Rather, there was a kind of anger against God. They had done their best to repay Him, but He had not kept His part of the deal, in making them feel rewarded.

There is the rather direct way of *scrupulosity*, trying to repay by meticulous, punctilious, solicitous, and rigorous observance of the law—divine laws, human laws, social and cultural laws. It was his recognition of this tendency in certain Christians which led the wise Sam Shoemaker to say, "The converts of one decade can so easily become the Pharisees of the next."

"But," you are saying, "aren't we supposed to live up to God's commandments and the principles of His Word? Aren't we expected to repay God with our service and our sacrifices?" And the answer to all such questions is a firm and positive, "Yes." *The issue here is the old problem of getting the cart before the horse. We are most certainly called to respond to grace with obedience and service and sacrifice. But we are not to do these things in order to earn God's grace, win His approval, or repay Him by trying to even up the credit-debit balance sheet. We now do these things because God loves us and accepts us as we are, because He freely forgives us and restores us into His family in spite of our undeservedness and unworthiness. We do them not in order to win His love, but out of gratitude for His love. Not in order to earn His grace, but out of thankfulness for it.*

The most basic Scripture on the subject, Ephesians 2,

ends with a verse which makes this crystal clear. "For we are God's workmanship, created in Christ Jesus to do good works, which God prepared in advance for us to do" (v. 10). The order of the horse and cart is very plain; we are saved not *by* good works but *for* good works. They are not the *root* of our salvation, but its *fruit*.

God's Unconditional Love

If we go back a few verses in Ephesians 2, we see the fountainhead of grace. "Because of His great love for us, God, who is rich in mercy, made us alive with Christ even when we were dead in transgressions—it is by grace you have been saved" (vv. 4-5). Grace is God's love in action toward those who do not deserve it. And this love is manifested as grace, offered us in the life and death of Christ. Hence God does not say,

I love you *because* . . .

I love you *since* . . .

I love you *forasmuch as* . . .

> or,

I will love you *if* . . .

I will love you *when* . . .

I will love you *after* . . .

I will love you *provided* . . .

I will love you *presuming* . . .

Any such statement would make His love *conditional*, would mean His love was caused by something in us—our attractiveness, our goodness, our lovableness. The reverse of this would mean there could be something in us which would stop God from loving us. *God's love for us is unconditional; it is not a love drawn from God by something good in us. It flows out of God because of His nature. God's love is an action toward us, not a reaction to us. His love depends not on what we are but on what He is. He loves because He is love.*

We can refuse the love of God, but we cannot stop Him

from loving us. We can reject it and thus stop its inflow into us, but we can do nothing to stop its outflow from Him. Grace is the unconditional love of God in Christ freely given to the sinful, the undeserving, and the imperfect.

I want to emphasize the word *imperfect* for the sake of performance-oriented Christians who often ask an important question. "But what if I fail? What if I fall?"

I will always remember a turning point in the spiritual life of one of the young teenagers of our church. He had already made his personal commitment to Christ. He tried hard but, like most adolescents, was plagued by the ups and downs in his Christian life. So he often came forward to the prayer altar during the invitation time following church services. He had done so once again after a Sunday night service conducted by a visiting evangelist. I had prayed with him and now we sat talking together at the altar. His face was very sober as he shared with me his determination "to make it this time." Then he asked, "But what if I fail? What happens if I fall?"

I replied, "Steve, I've come to know you pretty well. Probably better than anyone in the church. So I think I can guarantee you one thing—*you will fail, you will fall. So what?*"

He looked up at me a bit shocked. He had expected me to reassure him, not give him a guarantee of failure. When he didn't reply, I could see he was thinking over the implications of my "So what?"

And then something seemed to dawn on him. It was almost as if the rays from a flashlight had gradually moved across his face. Very slowly he began to smile and to nod his head. "Hmmm . . . I think I see what you mean. I think I'm catching on," he said. "Of course I'm going to fail; sure I'll fall. *But that really doesn't make any difference, does it?*" And then the smile lit up his whole face.

Of course, a lot of growth followed, but that was his

initial discovery of the way of grace. And his discovery—
that with grace, failure doesn't make any difference—
changed his life. It was a joy to watch him grow in grace.
Later, he became a dispenser of grace as a pastor for elev-
en years, and now teaches about grace as a professor of
systematic theology in a seminary. Are you wondering
about my strange reply that I was sure he would fail because I knew him so well? That's because I happen to be
his dad!

To ask the question, "What if I fail or fall?" is once
again to attach strings to God's unconditional love and to
change the nature of grace as *undeserved and unearnable
favor*. If our failure could stop grace, there would never be
any such thing as grace. For the ground of grace is the
cross of Christ, and on the cross we were *all* judged as *total
failures*. It was not a question of an occasional failure here
and there. As far as our ability to bridge the moral canyon
and win the approval of a holy God, *we are all total failures. In the Cross we were all examined and we all flunked
completely!*

This is what the first few chapters of Romans is all
about. Whether we are ethical do-gooders—the Jews—
who have kept all the commandments; or whether we are
out-and-out sinners who break them all—the Gentiles—
makes no difference. For God in His love has provided a
new basis for a right(eous) relationship with Him—free,
undeserved, unmerited, unrepayable favor, graciously offered to us. That's grace. And it's ours for the receiving.
That's faith. So the question of our failure or success
doesn't arise. The basis of salvation is not achieving but
receiving, not perfect performance but trusting faith.

"But now a righteousness from God, apart from Law,
has been made known, to which the Law and the Prophets testify. This righteousness from God comes through
faith in Jesus Christ to all who believe. There is no difference, for all have sinned and fall short of the glory of

God, and are justified freely by His grace through the redemption that came by Christ Jesus. . . . If by grace, then it is no longer by works [performance]; if it were, grace would no longer be grace" (Romans 3:21-24; 11:6).

Grace and the Heart

The basic difficulties for performance-minded Christians do not arise from the mind—reason and logic. Merely changing their mental concept of grace will not free them from the bondage of life on the performance grindstone. Grace may begin for them as a doctrinal concept, but it must become an experience which finally saturates their emotions as well. *Grace needs to be fully realized.* According to the dictionary, realization is "the act or process of becoming real." For this to happen, grace needs to penetrate and permeate the *heart.*

There is much misunderstanding about what the Scripture means by the heart. Misguided by our everyday use of the word, we have forgotten that *in the Bible heart means every area and function of the personality.*[2] H. Wheeler Robinson, an outstanding Bible scholar, analyzed the various senses in which the Hebrew and Greek words for *heart* are used:[3]

Sense	O.T.	N.T.
Personality	257	33
Emotional State	166	19
Intellectual Activity	204	23
Volition	195	22

It is extremely important to see how the word *heart* is used to express the personality as a whole or one of the functions of personality. It represents the selfhood, the central citadel of a person where thoughts, perceptions, feelings, decisions, and actions all influence each other, and are, in turn, influenced by the other.

There are places in the Bible where *heart* shows the person *in relationship*—both good and bad. Leviticus 19:17 warns against hating "your brother in your heart." Matthew 18:35 urges, "Forgive your brother from your heart." There are several verses which describe people who honor God "with their lips but their hearts are far from" Him (Isaiah 29:13; Matthew 15:8; Mark 7:6). Here the heart is shown in the degree of intimacy—its nearness or farness. Of course, passages which command, "Love the Lord your God with all your heart" imply a strong and close relationship with Him (Deuteronomy 6:5; Matthew 22:37). It was said that early Christians were "one in heart and mind," describing a relationship where "no one claimed that any of his possessions was his own, but they shared everything they had" (Acts 4:32). Paul expressed his special relationship to the Philippians when he said, "I have you in my heart" (Philippians 1:7). And he urges them to forgive one another and to be kind and "tenderhearted to one another" (Ephesians 4:32, KJV). It would not be too much to say that the heart is the fountainhead and source of our relational life. Grace in the heart is the spring out of which flows a grace-filled life. And this means *grace must touch feelings as well as concepts*. As William Kirwan says:

> Scripture regards the emotions of the heart as of great importance. Yet the place of emotions has been misunderstood by the evangelical Christian community. At best, emotions are merely tolerated. More often, they are treated as wrong or sinful. Indeed, much Christian theology has somehow gone awry on this key matter. . . . According to the Bible emotions and feelings have a clearly defined role in the Christian frame of reference. . . .
>
> "Facts" and "feelings" are part of the same process. The brain does not separate feelings from facts or

facts from feelings. There is little distinction between the two: all feelings are psychological and neurological arousal attached to facts. . . . Nor does the Bible make a distinction between facts and feelings. . . . We deal not with facts *or* feelings, but with facts *and* feelings. . . . By seeing emotions or feelings as a key aspect of the heart we see that they are also a key part of one's being. As a key to being, they are of vital importance in the life of the Christian.[4]

Doctrinal belief in a theology of grace, as important as that is, does not change the way performance-grounded Christians live. This is not understood by a large number of persons involved in Christian service—pastors, evangelists, teachers, and counselors, and so they sincerely but mistakenly deal with problems brought to them by parishioners only on a cognitive level—preaching/teaching/ admonishing. When this fails, the Christian worker—who is obviously in a position of authority over such persons— labels their problems as sin, rebellion, unbelief, disobedience, a lack of submission, self-centeredness, or the like. This only adds to the existing guilt, depression, and despair of the hurting person. I have wept over the letters, phone calls, and interviews describing such verbal bludgeoning by Christian workers in the name of Christ. I am sure God Himself weeps over these sincere but misguided efforts. Paul's words about the keepers of the Law are so fitting, "They are zealous for God, but their zeal is not based on knowledge" (Romans 10:2).

There is a better way—the all-encompassing way of grace.

- Healing grace for damaged emotions of the past
- Reconstructive grace for destructive interpersonal relationships
- Reprogramming grace for distorted personality patterns

● Recycling grace to transform cripplings into means of ministry.

In order to understand and experience this life of grace, we need to discover just how to apply this grace to the specific problems of guilt, low self-esteem, phoniness, anger, and poor personal relationships—all discussed in chapter 1.

"Wait a minute," someone protests. "I need help *right now*. As I've been reading, I've realized I need to do something about my problems, but I'm scared. *I need help just to get up the courage to face these things.*"

I've got good news for you. The same grace we've been describing can make you strong enough and brave enough to *take off your superself mask and begin to look at your real self*. For it's your real self which God loves and for which Christ died, your real self with all its sins and flaws which He has always known and never stopped loving. Feeling this at gut level gives you courage to face yourself as you truly are. I want to illustrate this with a remarkable true story that comes out of World War II.

There was a man named Stypulkowski who was a fighter in the Polish underground resistance movement from 1939 to 1944. Unfortunately, when the war ended he was in the wrong place at the wrong time and was captured by the Russian army. He and fifteen other Poles were taken to Russia to stand trial before their war crimes court. Since some Western observers were at the trials, it was necessary to get full confessions from the men in order to convict them of their supposed treason against the state. Actually, they had helped defeat the enemy with their tactics. Now, they were accused of helping the Nazis.

Prior to the trial, the men were put under rigorous interrogation to break them mentally, emotionally, and spiritually, to destroy their integrity so they would confess to anything demanded of them. Fifteen of the sixteen men broke under the grueling pressure. Only Stypulkowski didn't. And this in spite of the fact that for 69 out of 70 nights he was brutally questioned in a series of 141 interrogations. Not only did he endure them, but at one point his interrogator broke and had to be replaced. Over and over again his tormentors relentlessly examined everything he had ever done, or hadn't done—examined it for its fear and guilt content. His work, his marriage, family, children, his sex life, his church and community life, even his concept of God.

This followed weeks of a starvation diet, sleepless nights, and calculated terror. Most insidious of all were the signed confessions of his best friends, all of whom blamed him. His torturers told him his case was hopeless and as good as closed. They advised him to plead guilty so they could lessen his sentence; otherwise, it was certain death.

But Stypulkowski refused. He said he had not been a traitor and could not confess to something which was not true. He went on to plead not guilty at his trial; largely because of the foreign observers there, he was freed. Most impressive was the completely natural and unselfconscious way he witnessed to his Christian faith. He kept that faith alive by regular prayer, and every other loyalty was subordinated to his loyalty to Christ.

Oh, it was evident that he was not free from weaknesses—his accusers pointed them out to him time after time—but he was never shattered by them. The reason for his endurance was that he daily presented himself to God and to his accusers in absolute honesty. He knew he was accepted, loved of God, forgiven and cleansed. So whenever they accused him of some personal wrong, *he freely admitted it, even welcomed it.* Again and again he humbly said, "I never felt it necessary to justify myself with excuses. When they showed me I was a coward, I already knew it. When they shook their finger at me with accusations of filthy, lewd feelings, I already knew that. When they showed me a reflection of myself with all my inadequacies, I said to them, 'But gentlemen, *I am much worse than that.*' For you see, *I had learned it was unnecessary for me to justify myself. One had already done that for me—Jesus Christ!*"

Because Stypulkowski could be totally honest about himself before God, he was able to be totally honest about himself before his accusers. He could freely admit his personal failures because he knew they had all been taken care of in the Cross.

And so with all of us. When we realize that being "justified through faith, we have peace with God through our Lord Jesus Christ, through whom we have *gained access by faith into this grace in which we now stand*" (Romans 5:1), we will find the courage to face the truth about our needs, and experience healing grace.

Eight.

GRACE AND GUILT

Jesus, lover of my soul,
Let me to Thy bosom fly,
While the nearer waters roll,
While the tempest still is high;
Hide me, O my Saviour, hide,
Till the storm of life is past;
Safe into the haven guide;
O receive my soul at last!

Plenteous grace with Thee is found,
Grace to cover all my sin;
Let the healing streams abound;
Make and keep me pure within.
Thou of life the fountain art;
Freely let me take of Thee:
Spring Thou up within my heart;
Rise to all eternity.

*I*n chapter 1 we listed the commonest symptoms troubling Christians who are caught in the performance trap—guilt, low self-esteem, phoniness, anger, and difficulties with interpersonal relationships. It is not easy to separate these, because they are so closely interwoven in the pattern of an individual's lifestyle. To concentrate on just *one* of the problems is like trying to pull one loose strand out of a knitted garment, only to find the whole thing is unraveling.

It is this very intertwining which makes the fabric so strong and gives such persons their formidable defenses against change. I find it amazing how people will hang onto a problem, *even after they realize that it is the cause of their pain.* It's much too simple to say, "They enjoy suffering," for most of them don't. Their pain is genuine and they do not enjoy it. However, it is easier for them to hold onto something familiar, *with which they feel safe or comfortable—even though it hurts, than to let it go and face the unknown.* Change is *threatening to them;* they realize if they relinquish anything, *they will have to change their whole way of living.*

Often, during a time of deep healing prayer, the Holy Spirit draws back the curtain and the counselee will become aware of a decisive issue. It is literally as if God has put His finger on that one thread and wants their permission to remove it. But they know that if they allow Him to do that, their whole outfit will come to pieces. And how often I have heard them cry out in words similar to these, "But I can't give that up. I just can't. *It's the only thing I've got. It's the only thing that's really mine!*"

This is why, as we examine some of the various symptoms of life in the performance trap, as we look at some strands in the garment made without grace, we must again and again remind ourselves that it is an all-inclusive pattern. No one thread can be removed without affecting the overall design.

Global Guilt

Feelings of guilt, condemnation, and being disapproved by God are first on our list. This is because guilt is usually the driving force and chief motivator of such people. But exactly what is guilt? There are several meanings to the word and it will help if we sort them out. As with many other things in life, there is the good news and the bad news in regard to guilt.

The good news is that guilt is a form of mental pain; as any medical expert will tell you, pain is one of the best friends we have. It's the most valuable part of our built-in warning system. Dr. Paul Brand worked for many years among the lepers of India, and he became highly skilled in rehabilitation surgery. He would attempt to repair the disease-eaten hands of lepers so that they could earn a living after they were cured. He discovered the main problem was the fact that the lepers *felt no pain,* and so were always seriously injuring their hands or feet. After all kinds of experiments he further discovered there was no way to restore sensitivity to pain once it was destroyed, and so other means of warning had to be devised. Dr. Brand considers pain part of a brilliantly designed system and one of God's most amazing gifts to the human body. But he has also seen the other side of pain—its cruelty—as he has watched patients die in unbearable agony.

Guilt is a form of mental and emotional pain we experience when we feel responsible for doing, or not doing, something which violates our personal moral standard. In that sense, it too is a gift of God to fallen and sinful human beings, and is intended to be part of His restraining and redeeming grace. Persons who have no sense of guilt are considered abnormal. They are called sociopaths or psychopaths, and many of them are dangerous. In a sense they are moral and spiritual lepers who have lost the ability to feel the pain of guilt, even when they have violated the most basic moral standards or committed the most atrocious crimes. They are like Charlie Starkweather who in the 1950s went on a cross-country shooting spree and killed fourteen innocent victims. At his trial, when asked if he felt guilty, he replied, "No, it was just like shootin' rabbits!" He is an extreme example of someone without a conscience, without any ability to feel the pain of guilt.

But guilt can also go to the opposite extreme and become a cruel and destructive taskmaster. This is the kind of guilt so prevalent in the lives of performance-oriented Christians. For theirs is not the normal and specific feeling of guilt which comes when they have done or thought something wrong. Instead, it is a vague and generalized emotion. When I asked one counselee to describe his sense of guilt, he coined his own word to aptly describe it. "With me being guilty is a feeling of *alloverishness.*" This all-over guilt is what accounts for the *moral and spiritual drivenness* of such Christians. The constant pressure of their guilt keeps them trying to do and be more and more. Despite all the Scripture passages they know, and their many efforts to "trust and obey," they seem unable to shake off their feelings of guilt and to maintain an assurance that they are forgiven and acceptable to God. Let's try to sort out some of the reasons why these people find it so difficult to break free from the chains of guilt.

Victims of Victims

In chapter 4, while acknowledging that all human problems are the result of sin, we asked the question, "But whose sins?" One of the most basic steps in finding freedom from unnecessary guilt is to distinguish between taking responsibility for our own sins and refusing to take it for the sins done against us by other people. Research into alcoholism, wife abuse, child abuse, and sexual abuse shows there are many situations in which people are vic-

tims of victims. Unfortunately, one factor which perpetu-
ates such generational sins "unto the children's children"
is that many Christians do not break from the chains of
guilt associated with them.

One of the times I have been the angriest was many
years ago when a visiting evangelist preached a series of
meetings for the church I was pastoring. Dolores, a sincere
young woman who faithfully attended all the services, was
driven by deep feelings of guilt and went to counsel with
the evangelist. For the first time in her life she got up
nerve enough to tell about being sexually abused by her
father. It began when she was six and continued until she
was nine. Finally she could bear it no longer and told her
mother about it. Her mother became furious, gave her a
severe beating, and accused her of deliberately "seducing"
her father. With painful tears, Dolores shared the whole
story with the evangelist. Then she asked what she could
do to be free from the seemingly unresolvable feelings of
guilt. He told her she would never get rid of those feelings
"until she repented before God of her own responsibility
in the matter." She was utterly shattered by his advice and
came near to breaking under the newly added load of
guilt.

I marvel that Dolores ever came to see me—another
preacher. It's a tribute to her sheer desperation and the
grace of God. And I must confess I was so angry at that
evangelist I could hardly control myself. I've since learned
not to be shocked at the ghastly things which pass for
"Christian counseling" and "spiritual advice." It's amazing
how cruel some "helpers" can be, especially in the area of
heaping even greater guilt upon Christians who are just
barely surviving their present load.

Can you understand the layers of guilt Dolores had to
work through? Her mother accusing her of seduction; the
evangelist representing the voice of God and reinforcing
her mother's judgment of her. Again and again I tried to

point out to her how ridiculous it was to blame a six-year-old child for seducing a grown man. But always she would come back with, "I must have done something wrong." Or, "I shouldn't have crawled up into his lap and hugged him so much." She simply could not admit how wrong both her mother and dad had been and how deeply they had hurt her. She seemed intent on holding onto the guilt. Dolores was the perfect example of so many damaged Christians. *They would rather take all the blame for what someone did to them than face the truth about the persons who did it. This is especially true when the victimizers are people they want to love and respect—like parents, important relatives, teachers, preachers, or spouses.*

A vicious and nearly unbreakable circle of guilt is set up when we hold to the guilt. There seems no way out, because there's no way for God's grace to get in. His grace enters only when we forgive those who have sinned against us. And we can't really forgive them until we admit how much they've hurt us, and then face how we feel toward them. And that's impossible as long as we keep on taking responsibility for the sins they have committed.

The verse we frequently hear quoted from the Old Testament story of Joseph, as he forgave his brothers, is "You intended to harm me, but God intended it for good" (Genesis 50:20). This is a great verse, and we rightfully emphasize the last part of the verse. But we must not overlook the first part, "You intended to harm me." Joseph squarely faced up to the evil his brothers had done. He did not minimize or excuse it. Many people today mistakenly think that forgiveness means to overlook the evils done against them; they feel they are being sweet, loving Christians. Actually, this is an exercise in unreality which keeps out the power of grace.

Furthermore, it is the Holy Spirit, the Spirit of Truth, who activates God's grace in our lives. As long as we are dishonest and untruthful in our hearts, He cannot free us from our feelings of guilt and give us lasting peace. This is why we often need a pastor, counselor, or some other temporary assistant to the Holy Spirit to help us sort out true and false guilt. Of course, it also means that when we get it sorted out, we need to take full responsibility for our own sins. With Dolores, this meant acknowledging how badly she had been hurt by the betrayal of her parents. Then she needed to forgive them, *and ask God to forgive her for resenting them for what they had done to her.* In this way true forgiveness for real guilt—*both theirs and hers*—could and did take place. It was the beginning of a new life of inner peace for Dolores.

Though the details of your story may be entirely different from hers, this process of sorting out true responsibility and actual guilt may be where you need to start your pilgrimage of grace. For in our lives, as in the life of Jesus, "grace and truth" always go together (John 1:14).

False Guilt

There are situations where we need to distinguish true from false guilt. One of the ways a child's conscience develops ideas of right and wrong is to internalize the standards of people he considers important. He wants them to approve of him, and so he gradually incorporates their values and makes them his own. This process rightly handled is the basis of a Christian home and of bringing up children in the discipline and instruction of the Lord. It is also the foundation of Christian education in Sunday School, youth group, and church. When these standards are based on Scripture, rooted in loving relationships, and reinforced by consistent example, a healthy Christian conscience will result.

But this God-designed process can also be the means of developing a damaged, supersensitive conscience which can plague Christians with an overwhelming sense of guilt. Sometimes this happens because there is an excessive emphasis on minor rules and regulations within the family or church; or when the discipline and punishment for breaking the rules is far out of proportion to their importance. Legalistic, graceless homes, churches, or communities often produce warped consciences which entrap Christians in guilt. Years ago one of my mentors told me something I have seen confirmed by a lifetime of counseling. He said, "Whenever you see excess scrupulosity, look out for emotional damage."

All this becomes even more serious when such overconscientiousness is *enforced by emotional or spiritual blackmail. That is, when guilt is used to control or manipulate people.* This blackmail can build into them a destructive sense of false guilt which can keep them on a performance treadmill for many years.

Cliff was one of the most guilt-ridden persons I've ever met. He was a spiritual workaholic with an obsession to be constantly busy for the Lord. Accompanying this was a feeling that it was impossible to relax his efforts even for a moment, because this would not be pleasing to God. He had a strange sense of always being watched. He carried an almost unbearable burden for the souls of people he contacted—their eternal destiny was his responsibility. He was sure that if he failed them, their blood would be on his hands. Several times he had been saved from the brink of emotional breakdown by some close friends who practically forced him to take a few days rest and gave him a lot of loving support. But this had actually added to his sense of guilt in the long run—God must be even more displeased and disappointed because he hadn't kept on trying.

It took a while for Cliff to stop flagellating himself and to share with me the picture of his family history. It was saturated with emotional and spiritual blackmail—as happens when none of the ordinary forms of discipline or physical punishments are employed to confront misbehavior or maintain family order. Instead, sympathy, disapproval, and guilt are used as emotional pressure points to dictate even the most insignificant family behavior. Cliff's mother carried a heavy martyr complex and used every possible means to control the family with her illnesses and nervous ailments. These required a constant round of doctors—the actual causes could never be found—to prescribe the rest and medicines which kept her going. Cliff was the eldest child who took the brunt of it, and very early got overloaded with some heavy burdens. "I felt I had to be perfect and help keep the other kids in line, because we were all poor Mother had. And I had to work extra hard to keep any load off her. After all, she was suffering enough from some terrible disease—probably a hidden cancer they couldn't locate—and from a husband who, though in front of others acted like he cared, behind the scenes was inconsiderate and worthless. A phrase we heard constantly was, 'You'll never know what I've had to put up with from your father, but that's part of a wife's duty.' All of us children presumed this to be a sexual reference."

There was also more direct spiritual blackmail, for everything had a religious connotation. To obey and please her was to obey and please God; to disobey her was to get God's frowning disapproval. By now Cliff's voice was filled with emotion. "In my mind God and Mom became the same. I see that now. And I desperately wanted to love and please them both—I mean her and God. But there was no way to love Mom. I don't think she really wanted love. She just wanted lots of sympathy for her physical sufferings, and for being married to Dad. And you couldn't please her because her needs kept changing. Poor Dad. I know now I never really saw him except through her eyes. He was actually a patient and rather wonderful guy."

Gradually Cliff began to realize it wasn't God who was always watching him. It wasn't God who kept looking over his shoulder to criticize every book he read, to question every opinion he voiced, and to disapprove of every activity or relationship in which he was involved. Yes, *it seemed like God, felt like God, sounded like God, but it wasn't. It was the voice of an unpredictable and unpleasable mother which had become internalized into his conscience.* It was so deep with Cliff that he had now joined the watchers club himself, introspecting everything about his spiritual life. When he prayed or read the Bible or witnessed, it was as if he was always watching himself praying, reading, or witnessing. Cliff reminded me of an absurd story I heard about a window cleaner on a New York skyscraper, who stepped back to look at his work! Funny? Not in Cliff's case, for there were times he almost destroyed himself by his endless introspection.

It took a long time for us to work through the many layers of Cliff's guilt. Insight into his family system helped him understand much about both himself and his parents. He needed this not so he could blame anyone, but in order to learn how to forgive and love. It also helped for us to go over a lot of the do's and don'ts together. He needed reassurance and encouragement as he learned how to vote against his own guilty feelings. This is often impossible to do on our own. *Though we may know we are right, the old voices of guilt make us feel so wrong they almost tear us to pieces.* So we must have the support of a person or a group, as one necessary step. However, the ultimate solution does not lie in just rectifying the rules, or distinguishing between God's revealed standards and internalized human opinions.

Neither does it lie in another direction—something which most counselors have had to learn the hard way. Freedom and joy would not come by my taking the place of his mother and becoming a surrogate parent or authority figure telling Cliff how to live. It's easy for Christian workers to fall into that kind of dependency trap. When this happens the cure becomes a part of the disease itself. Remember, we are only *temporary assistants* to the Holy Spirit. The ultimate goal is to help people receive their support from the body life of the church and their counseling directly from the Great Counselor, the Holy Spirit.

The deepest damage in Cliff, and many others like him who come out of such parental dysgrace, is their *unscriptural and dysgraceful concept of God.* Theirs is not the gracious God who is revealed to us in Jesus Christ. He is an unstable, unreasonable, and above all, unpleasable God whose acceptance and love we have to earn by perfect performance. Along with this, they have an unbiblical and dysgraceful concept of a right relationship with God. This naturally follows, for a wrong concept of God leads to a faulty concept of what God wants from us. And a faulty concept of what He wants from us leads to a skewed idea of how He relates to us and wants us to relate to Him. So Cliff and I worked together, allowing the Spirit to peel away several layers of distorted concepts and to heal many damaged emotions. This process reminded me of a time when a doctor informed me I needed a major operation, but that before he could operate, several secondary infections had to be cleared up.

And so it was with Cliff. He had certainly come a long way. The cruel intensity of his former feelings of guilt were gone, and he was a much more winsome witness for Christ. But he could not really get away from the overarching sense of God's disapproval. After hearing a Sunday sermon on "Resting in the Lord," he told me with a nervous laugh that his Christian life could more aptly be titled "Walking on Eggshells!" He was still living as if God's approval depended on *his* performance rather than on Christ's perfection.

In some ways, all our sorting out of real and pseudoguilt

had made matters worse for him. For Christians—and please remember this is being addressed to Christians—it's not possible to solve the guilt problem for another by saying, "For this you ought to feel guilty" and "For this you don't need to feel guilty." It is not our business to condemn them for what may seem to us as a failure to live up to the demands of the law. The moment we condemn, *we are then saying we believe the opposite, that is, that we have the ability to justify ourselves by performing all the works of the law.* That is a gospel of works and not of grace. For grace is the good news that right relatedness to God no longer depends on our ability to keep the law. Rather, it depends on fully admitting we are not able to do so. Better still, we no longer need to do so. Instead, we become rightly related to God by what He has done for us in Christ. "For Christ means the end of the struggle for righteousness by the Law for everyone who believes in Him" (Romans 10:4, PH).

At this point I asked Cliff to read and reread Romans in an up-to-date translation. When we next met together, he was visibly shaken. "This business of grace is getting to me," he said, "and I must confess I'm confused. Actually my guilt seems worse, and I don't like that. But it seems to be a different kind of guilt." And then Cliff told me an interesting story. "I'm not sure I understand all this. Anyhow, recently when I was singing 'Amazing Grace,' two lines struck me afresh. 'Twas grace that taught my heart to fear, and grace my fears relieved.' I stopped singing and was thinking about the paradox in those words when very quietly inside me, it seemed that God had put His loving arms around me and was saying, 'Cliff, I accept you and love you just the way you are right now.' I've never experienced such a feeling of unconditional love. It was incredible. But immediately I felt myself getting upset, and inwardly I said to God almost angrily, *'Well, You may accept me, but I don't. After all, I have my standards!'* "

Because Cliff had expressed his thoughts out loud, he heard and understood what he had actually said. And it shocked him into the realization of what *sin, guilt, grace,* and *salvation* really mean. Sin and guilt are the *core* of the disease; grace and salvation are the *cure*. And only the Holy Spirit can ultimately bring this about within us. For while our *conscience* accuses us of violating our moral standards, or the *internalized voices of dysgrace* fill us with all kinds of false guilt, *the Holy Spirit* does not condemn us because we have failed to be good. He convicts us, says Jesus, "about sin, because men do not believe in Me" (John 16:8-9). Grace brings us to the place of *real guilt,* real guilt for our only real sin—failing to believe in Jesus Christ and trust Him for right relatedness to God. This is what happened to Cliff in that moment when he realized it was not his many sins nor his sense of badness which kept him from finding peace with God. It was *his pride, his sense of goodness.* Pride which, in an unguarded moment of honesty, had actually told God that Cliff's way of righteousness by performance was better than God's way of unconditional grace.

Grace solves the problem of guilt not in a piecemeal manner, but by giving us a whole new ground of relating to God through Christ and His cross. Grace means that God receives sinners. This is what shocked the good people of Jesus' day. "The Pharisees and the teachers of the law muttered, 'This Man welcomes sinners and eats with them' " (Luke 15:2). The Pharisees were the most morally righteous people in the land, obsessive in their devotion to keeping the Law. Yet Jesus told His disciples their righteousness must "surpass" that of the Pharisees, if they were to enter the kingdom of heaven (Matthew 5:20). What was it that distinguished the disciples from the Pharisees? It was not that the disciples were morally admirable and the Pharisees were not. Judging from the descriptions, it was quite the contrary, for the moral sins of the Pharisees were hidden, while the failures of the disciples were openly portrayed. The difference was in their relationship to Jesus. The disciples were with Jesus, joined to Him, while the Pharisees were not. The gospel of grace says this trust relationship to Christ is the only solution to the problem of guilt. For "there is now no condemnation for those who are in Christ Jesus" (Romans 8:1).

Nine.

GRACE AND
EMOTIONS

And can it be that I should gain an interest in the Saviour's blood?
Died He for me, who caused His pain?
For me, who Him to death pursued?
Amazing love! how can it be
That Thou, my God, shouldst die for me?

He left His Father's throne above, so free, so infinite His grace,
Emptied Himself of all but love
And bled for Adam's helpless race!
'Tis mercy all, immense and free,
For O my God, it found out me.

No condemnation now I dread: Jesus, and all in Him, is mine!
Alive in Him, my living Head,
And clothed in righteousness divine,
Bold I approach the eternal throne,
And claim the crown through Christ, my own.

Performance-oriented Christians generally feel low self-esteem. What do we mean by self-esteem? It is a mental image of ourselves, a collage of pictures including our *past* memories, our *present* situations, and our imaginary *futures*. All kinds of reflections, evaluations, and feelings accompany the pictures, forming a 3-D collage in living color and stereophonic sound, and generating within us certain feelings about ourselves. If those evaluations and emotions are mostly positive, we say we have a good self-image or feel good about ourselves. If they are largely negative, we say we have a bad self-image. When people come to counsel, one of the first things they share is the way they feel about themselves. Their expressions of low self-esteem range from a mild, "I don't like myself," to a vehement, "I just can't stand myself."

During World War II, a social worker helped evacuate children from London's dangerous bombing areas, taking them by bus out to the safer countryside. One day, as she lifted a four-year-old boy from the bus, she asked him, "Son, tell me your name." The lad looked up sadly and said, "Mum, I ain't nobody's nothin." Judging by their self-evaluations, that's the way many people feel about themselves.

But why is this so common among Christians? After all, it runs counter to every biblical doctrine about being adopted into God's family, becoming His children and joint heirs with Christ. If self-esteem were purely a matter of mental beliefs, Christians ought to stand taller and feel better about themselves than any other group of people. Why do so many genuinely reborn Christians suffer—and I do mean suffer—the pain of low self-esteem?

Self-Denial and Self-Worth
Many people are thoroughly confused about what it means to have a healthy Christian self-image. They've got self,

self-crucifixion, self-denial, self-respect, self-esteem, self-love, self-surrender, humility, pride, and a host of other related words, mixed in a tangled mass. Perhaps we should say mess, for it certainly messes up daily Christian living.

I'm thinking of two women in midlife who came for help. Barbara felt so guilty about the fact she couldn't "get rid of herself" that every time she used the word "I" she would stop and apologize. Finally she tried to eliminate "I" from the conversation entirely. Of course, it was utterly ludicrous as well as impossible. She felt very defeated when I pointed out that this effort was not only making her more self-centered but also making me more conscious of her than ever. She had recently heard a severe sermon on "crucifying self" based on Galatians 2:20. When I asked her to slowly read the verse out loud and count the number of "I's" and "me's" on her fingers as she read, she was quite astounded to find seven of them. The most self-surrendering verse in the New Testament turns out to be the most self-filled!

The second woman, Judith, came to see that her misunderstanding of self-esteem was destroying her and her marriage. As an individual she had been denying her God-given gifts; and as a wife she had failed to express herself to her husband and so had become resentful toward him. Why? She was afraid of being proud and felt the only way to prevent it was to deny and crucify herself. This meant she must consider herself of little or no value, keep reminding herself of her worthlessness, and constantly belittle herself. She thought this was humility.

The phrase, "Love your neighbor as yourself," occurs in the Bible nine times; once the command regards "the alien in your land . . . to love him as yourself." This adds up to twice by Moses (Leviticus 19:18; 19:34), five times by Jesus (Matthew 19:19; 22:39; Mark 12:31, 33; Luke 10:27), twice by Paul (Romans 13:9; Galatians 5:14) and once by James (2:8). Now it is technically true to say that we are not actually commanded in these Scriptures to love ourselves. *But the plain inference in every one of them is that a proper kind of self-love is the normal basis of relating to others.* It's not commanded, but it is assumed. Perhaps it's not commanded because it's just presumed that the people to whom they are speaking would love themselves and therefore should make that the norm by which they evaluated their love for others. This is certainly the presupposition of Paul's advice to husbands in Ephesians 5:28-29. "In this same way, husbands ought to love their wives as their own bodies. He who loves his wife loves himself. After all, no one ever hated his own body, but he feeds and cares for it, just as Christ does the church." The Scriptures *everywhere* assume that an appropriate self-love, self-care, and self-appreciation is normal, and *nowhere* tell us to hate or neglect ourselves, or to indulge in self-depreciation.

Self-denial consists in denying not our self-worth but our self-will, and in abandoning our search for self-glory. The crucifixion of the self is our willingness to renounce our carnal, self-glorifying self and allow it to be put to death on the cross with Christ. It does not mean we renounce or belittle our God-given gifts; it does mean we surrender them to God to be used for His glory. Pride, as it is used in the Bible, is a dishonest estimate of ourselves. Paul warns against this, "For by the grace given to me I say to every one of you, Do not think of yourself more highly than you ought, but rather think of yourself with sober judgment, in accordance with the measure of faith God has given you" (Romans 12:3). Just as Paul reminds us we are saved by grace through faith and that not of ourselves, he here reminds us that God's grace and our faith will also give us an honest and accurate estimate of ourselves. In both instances, pride is excluded, because the grace and the faith are both gifts from God. As Paul so incisively asks, "For who makes you different from anyone else? What do you have that you did not receive? And if you did receive it, why do you boast as though you did not?" (1 Corinthians 4:7)

Someone once asked Corrie ten Boom how she could possibly handle all the compliments and praise that were constantly heaped upon her, without becoming proud. She said she looked at each compliment as a beautiful long-stemmed flower given to her. She smelled it for a moment and then put it into a vase with the others. Each night, just before retiring, she took the beautiful bouquet and handed it over to Jesus saying, "Thank You, Lord, for letting me smell the flowers; they all belong to You." She had discovered the secret of genuine humility.

Humility means that while I like myself and appreciate the affirmation of others, I don't need to prove my worth to God, myself, or others. Healthy Christian self-esteem rests on the firm foundation of *knowing we are accepted, loved, and appreciated by God Himself.* This generates in us a humility which is born out of gratitude for His undeserved grace and which comes from God. Feelings of inferiority, insecurity, and inadequacy do not come from God, but from Satan, as a counterfeit for true humility.

Barriers to Grace

However, as in the case of guilt, many Christians completely agree with all this and yet are still plagued by a sense of worthlessness and low self-esteem. In spite of constant efforts to memorize the right verses, think positively, and "become who they are in Christ," at a gut level they are unable to feel good about themselves. Let us look at several inner barriers to grace.

• The need to forgive ourselves. Many Christians suffer from recurring bouts of self-despising because they have not truly forgiven themselves for past moral failures. They say, "Yes, I am a Christian. I believe Christ died for my sins and so I believe God has forgiven me. But way down deep I'm spiritually kicking myself for something. I keep a slow-motion video replay of it running and end up berating and belittling myself."

We have already referred to the story of Joseph forgiving his brothers. There are several very remarkable incidents in the story. One which shows Joseph's unusual sensitivity is described in Genesis 45. Joseph, struggling with his own racking emotions, had just revealed himself to his brothers, who "were terrified at his presence." They remembered their heinous crime against him and realized he could have had them all executed. And in that tumultuous moment, Joseph could have turned in on himself and been overwhelmed by his own emotions. Instead, with an incredible insight into human nature, he realized his brothers were going to have a hard time *really believing in and accepting his forgiveness.* So he turned from any concern for himself to concern for them, wanting to help them *receive his forgiveness.* He said to them, "I am your brother, Joseph, the one you sold into Egypt! And now, *do not be distressed and do not be angry with yourselves* for selling me here, because it was to save lives that God sent me ahead of you" (Genesis 45:5, italics added). Joseph was saying, "Don't hate yourselves for what you did. Not only do I forgive you for it, but better still, God took your evil and worked it all out for good—even *your* good."

If that's what Joseph could say to his brothers, *how much more does Christ, our Elder Brother, say to all of us,* "Don't keep on being distressed and hating yourselves for some past sin. I have suffered and died for all your sins, including that one. Show that you accept My gift of forgiveness by forgiving yourselves. When you keep on despising yourselves for your sins, you are not only insulting My death on the cross, but you are also in effect declaring that *the power of your sins is greater than the power of God; that you and your sins are so powerful God cannot work them out for* good. You are actually reversing God's Word to make it say, "Where grace abounded, sin superabounded!"

This is one area where special kinds of healing prayer are often needed.[1] In this type of Christian therapy we attempt to visualize Jesus ministering to persons at the time and place of their need. This visualizing is not a creation of our human imaginations. It is always biblically based, recreating some actual metaphor of Christ, or an incident from His life as pictured in the Gospels. Let me share one woman's experience of full forgiveness through the healing of something in her past which had kept her bound.

It helped me to identify some painful memories that have blocked my growth spiritually for a long time. I had been dealing with "that sinful woman in my past" by throwing stones at her all these years. I was helped to walk back in my past in specific situations with Jesus. His response was, "Woman, where are your accusers? I don't accuse you either; go and sin no more." I am now responding to myself as Jesus would in every situation. He makes a much better Lord and Saviour than I do. . . . It has become so much easier these past few months to accept the "Saviour" side of Jesus. It's still hard to accept Him as "Lord." But I've been helped to look at my difficulty with authority figures and can see real progress of healing in that area too.

• The need to realize we don't need negative feelings anymore. Often when I ask Christians why they so obstinately hold onto their combination of past guilt and present self-disdain, they answer, "If I didn't feel that way toward myself, I'd probably fall back into open sin. I *need it to hold me in line.* There's no telling what I might do without it."

What a tragic misconception of the place of guilt and self-condemnation in the life of the Christian. There is a strong place for both in the lives of those outside Christ. That is the chief purpose of the Law in their lives—not to save them by obedience to it, but to reveal to them their sins, create within them a sense of guilty condemnation and lostness, and thus *drive them to their only hope in Christ.*

Therefore no one will be declared righteous in His sight by observing the law; rather, through the law we become conscious of sin. . . . Before this faith came, we were held prisoners by the law, locked up until faith should be revealed. So the law was put in charge to lead us to Christ that we might be justified by faith. Now that faith has come, we are no longer under the supervision of the law (Romans 3:20; Galatians 3:23-25).

Once we are in Christ, guilt, condemnation, and self-despising are no longer intended to be our chief motivators for righteous living. It will take time to change but sooner or later, love is to become the motivating force of our Christian living.

Is there then no place for the law? Has it been repealed? What does Paul mean when he says we are "not under law but under grace"? (Romans 6:14-15) Jesus said He came to fulfill the law (Matthew 5:17); so in what sense are we Christians free from it? According to Paul we are free from its *curse* (Galatians 3:13), its *compulsive power* (Romans 7:7-9), and its *demanding rituals* (Galatians 5:1-6). *But we are not free from its moral intentions toward God, ourselves, and other people.* However, these are now fulfilled in an entirely different way, "that the righteous requirements of the law might be fully met in us, who do not live according to the sinful nature but according to the Spirit" (Romans 8:4). "Therefore, love is the fulfillment of the law" (Romans 13:10).

146

From a *biblical* view, Christians who hang onto guilt, condemnation, and self-belittling worthlessness are living under the curse, the sting, and the power of the law. This is so readily observable from a psychological viewpoint. The idea that fear and guilt and self-condemnation will keep us from sinning and therefore give us inner peace and joy is completely contrary to experience. Those who live that way are filled with inner turmoil and driven by strong—even strange and seemingly uncontrollable—compulsions toward the very sins they try the hardest to avoid. Why? Because guilt and self-condemnation were never intended to be the motivating force of Christian living. The underlying emotion in guilt and self-hate is *fear. And fear is actually the most self-centered of all emotions. So when we use it as an appeal to righteous living, it only makes us more self-centered and anxious. Thus it defeats its own purpose and keeps us from the goal we are trying to attain.*

Guilt and self-despising are short-term motivators, intended to shake us out of our sins and get us moving toward Christ. But they are very poor long-term motivators. They may be all right for the 100-yard dash, but the Christian life is more like the 26-mile marathon which we are to "run with perseverance" (Hebrews 12:1).

Through the years I have seen the *liberating* power of Christ. To use the words of Charles Wesley's hymn, "He breaks the power of canceled sin, He sets the prisoner free."

But I've also seen the other side of the coin—the *captivating and restraining* power of His love and grace. In another well-known hymn, Robert Robinson writes of this aspect of grace.

> O to grace how great a debtor
> Daily I'm constrained to be!
> Let Thy goodness, like a fetter,
> Bind my wandering heart to Thee;

Prone to wander, Lord, I feel it,
Prone to leave the God I love,
Here's my heart, O take and seal it,
Seal it for Thy courts above.

Through the years I've observed when the chips are down, it is not guilty fear or self-condemnation that holds us steady. It is rather the visceral knowledge of God's unconditional grace and love for us. In Thomas Chalmers' phrase, it is "the expulsive power of a new affection."

Grace That Leads to Home

Evelyn's full story would fill many pages, for God had literally salvaged her out of a trash bin. Verbal, physical, and sexual abuse marked her youth. A teenage marriage to escape from home had only exchanged one set of problems for another. Soon she found herself a young divorcee trying to fill an almost insatiable need for male attention and love by going from one affair to another. And then, a Christian coworker introduced her to a warm, loving fellowship group, and she was dramatically converted. She felt God would have her finish her education. It was while a student in college that she came for counseling. In addition to the wounds of her early years, some of her own past sins had left deep scars on her life. Slowly but surely, God's saving, sanctifying, and healing grace brought remarkable changes to Evelyn's personality. The one area where she knew she must "watch and pray" the most was about her almost compulsive need for men. She realized she was, in a sense, still looking for a father.

Evelyn graduated and got a fine job as a secretary. Because she was conscientious and hard-working, she climbed the ladder and was named personal assistant to the head of the company. This meant many hours spent together at work and after hours. Although he was a married man with a family, she felt herself being drawn into an emotional closeness to him. It was never mentioned, but they both sensed what was happening.

One day, when he asked her to accompany him on a business trip, she knew down deep in her heart what this meant. She prayed and wept about it before God, but that old emptiness seemed to be drawing her into a vortex from which she couldn't escape.

On their second night out, while they were eating dinner, her boss expressed his feelings for her. She responded by telling him she felt the same way. She accepted his invitation and agreed to come to his room after the final business sessions were over. During the evening sessions, a terrific struggle took place in her. Later she wrote:

It was like a tug-of-war and I was the rope! By the time it was over, I was shaking like a leaf. Then it seemed as if a great inner peace took over. It really was "the peace that passeth understanding," because I certainly couldn't understand what I did. But as we walked out of the meeting together, I stopped and said, "Jim, I admire you more than any man I know. I want to be with you tonight so much I'm actually aching. It's my fault for leading you on. Forgive me. But you know, during the meeting I remembered something. *I remembered that a man from Kentucky told me how much God loved me, and I believed him. And I just can't go against that kind of love. It's done too much for my life and means too much to me."*

Evelyn had found the secret—the realization of God's unconditional love and undeserved grace that holds us steady in temptation. Not guilt and self-condemnation, but grace and its accompanying sense of self-worth.

Through many dangers, toils and snares

149

I have already come;
'Tis grace hath brought me safe thus far,
And grace will lead me home.

Did you ever notice that New Testament appeals for righteous, holy living are not *legal but relational?* Even in those passages with long lists of sins, guilt is not intended to keep the Christian in check. Almost always there is an appeal to a personal grace/love relationship. It's the same basis for commandment-keeping which Jesus gave, "If you love Me, you will obey what I command" (John 14:15). Too many Christians reverse this to mean, "If you keep all My commands, then I'll love you—maybe." Since we have the Holy Spirit living in us, the loving appeal to ethical living is powerful. How can we sin against the Spirit and risk hurting our relationship with Him?

We are told in Ephesians 4:30, "And do not *grieve* the Holy Spirit of God, with whom you were sealed for the day of redemption." And in 1 Thessalonians 5:19, "*Quench* not the Spirit" (KJV). In Ephesians 5:18, "Do not get drunk on wine, which leads to debauchery. Instead, be filled with the Spirit." This means we are not to *substitute intoxicating spirits for the Spirit's infilling.* The appeal is not to fear/guilt/condemnation to keep us from sin, but to a love/grace/gratitude relationship with the Person of God's Spirit. It's not, "Don't break an impersonal commandment," but, "Don't harm a loving personal relationship."

The notion that we must hold onto our guilt and self-despising in order to keep from sinning, and to have motivation for Christian living, is not biblical. It is usually a hangover from a previous period in our lives, when those very emotions were forms of conditional acceptance used to "keep us in line." This carryover leads to aspects of low self-esteem which come from damaged emotions. We will consider these in our next chapter and see how grace can bring healing and wholeness.

Ten.

GRACE AND
SELF-ESTEEM

O let me commend my Saviour to you,
I set my seal that Jesus is true:
Ye all may find favor who come to His call;
O come to the Saviour! His grace is for all.

Then let us submit His grace to receive,
Fall down at His feet and gladly believe:
We all are forgiven for Jesus' sake;
Our title to heaven His merits we take.

*I*n December of 1985, syndicated columnist Bob Greene wrote an article concerning a twelve-year-old boy who received a cruel card from his classmates. The card, manufactured and distributed by the Topps Chewing Gum Company, was headlined, "Most Unpopular Student Award." The boy's classmates had written his name on the card and left it on his desk. Greene had originally written about this because he felt it was wrong for a company to sell that kind of card. Topps dismissed his criticism, saying it was just a form of satire and innocent "insult humor." But the boy's teacher and school principal said it was causing him a lot of emotional damage. What amazed and impressed Greene the most was the avalanche of mail which came from his adult readers, telling of the lasting hurts they were still carrying around as a result of such "innocent" childhood incidents. Most of the people still were troubled by a sense of low self-esteem— even when they were elderly. That column was entitled, "The Pain That Never Goes Away."

The only thing in Greene's column that surprised me was his surprise. In May of 1986, I heard George Gallup, Jr. say his latest poll showed that one-third of Americans suffer from low self-esteem. He considered it to be the chief psychological malady of our day.

Let us see how we can cooperate with grace to remove the inner barriers which keep us from being healed of this painful malady.

The Deadly "I Am's"

If we are truly reborn children of God, our sense of worthlessness and low self-esteem does not come from Him— the One who called Himself the Great I Am. Instead it comes from our own deadly I am's. Let me explain.

Remember how we observed that the home is like a mirror in which we develop our self-concepts? How we come to see ourselves, and to value—or devalue—ourselves will be based largely on the evaluations of significant people in our lives. This is especially true in the early years of our development. There is no doubt there are inborn differences between children. From their very birth some children are highly sensitive and have a built-in radar that picks up the most minute details of home life. Others are born with an entirely different kind of receiving antenna which seems to screen out the static.

While these differences determine the *degree* to which children respond, there are some basic God-given needs which are the same for everyone. I am convinced that *the most serious single consequence of parental dysgrace is deeply damaged self-esteem.* Whether it has been done intentionally or unintentionally, indirectly or directly, negatively by deprivation or positively by rejection, the result is a sense of worthlessness and low self-esteem. *The perceived "You are's" of the parents become the inner "I am's" of the children.* I do not want to limit this to parents or stepparents, because other family members, neighbors, peers, teachers, and church personnel also play a major role. However, there is no doubt parents are the main ones involved. It is not that they necessarily word their rejection and say, "You are this" or "You are that." The message is given by their overall personalities, their inner and outer bearing and demeanor, by the radar they send out.

The *King James Version* of the Bible uses an old English word, *conversation,* which doesn't mean simply speaking with words, but indicates manner of life. The basic idea behind the word is the message being spoken to others by one's whole manner of living. It is this *conversation*—attitudes, actions, facial expressions, tones of voice, habitual responses, *or the lack of them*—which give us the "You are" messages which slowly but surely become the "I am's" of our lives. Long after the original people are gone—through distance, divorce, or even death—the powerful

"I am's" continue to be the painful source of our self-belittling or self-despising. As Bob Greene discovered, they can literally affect us for all of life.

In my book, *Putting Away Childish Things*, I dealt with these "I am's" as childhood mottoes which cripple adult behavior, mottoes such as "Measure up," "Brave boys don't cry," and "You'll never make it." Since then, people have given me many more of these put-downs which they say helped them form a low opinion of themselves.

You've no right to feel that way.
If you can't say something nice, don't say anything.
Why do you always do things like that?
If there's a wrong way to do it, you'll find it.
What makes you so stupid? clumsy? dumb? slow? silly?
All you gotta' do is use your head once in a while.
I can't believe you did such a thing.
Why can't you be more like your sister? brother?
I hate to think of how you'll turn out.
You're going to turn out to be just like _____
What in the world is wrong with you?
What does Jesus think about you when you do that?
God can't love naughty little boys/girls/kids.
Now *you'll* have to be the man/woman of the house.
Don't let anyone know what you're really like.
Why couldn't you have been a boy? a girl?
You were trouble before you were born.
You've been nothing but trouble since you were born.
I wish you'd never been born.
The only reason we stay together is because of you.
If I thought you were really sorry, I might forgive you.
I'm sick of you. or, You make me sick.
How could you do that after all we've done for you?
You shoulda' known better than to trust a man/woman.
Can't you do anything right?
No wonder you don't have any friends!

Notice that most of these statements are not criticisms or corrections of doing, but of being. This is extremely important in relation to our self-esteem. Psychologists who have made special studies of affirmation have come up with a formula about positive and negative strokes.

A positive stroke enhances us as persons. If it was given for *doing*—what *you did*—it's worth 1 point. If it was given for *being*—*what you are*—it's worth 10 points.

A negative stroke diminishes us as persons. If it was given for *doing*, it counts 10 points. If it was given for *being*, it counts 100 points!

My counseling experience confirms this formula. People will remember a single hurtful criticism most vividly, while tending to forget a string of compliments. And they will feel a positive or a negative statement about *what they are* much more deeply than one concerning *what they did*. Thus it's easy to see why the put-downs of *being* can be so completely shattering to our self-esteem. They hurt us not simply on the outside, for our behavior; but they pierce right into the inside of us, where the *concepts and feelings about ourselves originate*.

If these were simply isolated statements, occasionally uttered by exhausted and exasperated parents who were normally fair and loving, they would not be so harmful. But when they represent the general attitude and atmosphere of the home, the effect on self-image can be serious. Every one of them is a basic message which in one way or another says, *"You are worthless, you are bad, you are guilty, you are a failure, and you won't make it in life."* These "You are's" can become a permanent part of our "I am's"—the inner voice of our self-image—which then says, *"I am worthless, I am bad, I am guilty, I am a failure, and I won't make it in life."*

In their excellent book, *The Blessing*, Gary Smalley and John Trent maintain that our emotional and psychological makeup is such that we all need what the Bible calls "the blessing." This is the knowledge that someone in this world loves and accepts us unconditionally. Because our parents are so important to us during our formative years, we especially crave their blessing, and are hurt if we don't receive it. Smalley and Trent detail the five biblical elements of the blessing: meaningful touch, the spoken word, the expression of high value, the description of a special future, and the application of genuine commitment.

Here, indeed, is a fine description of what we have called parental grace. Contrast this with the verbal expressions of parental dysgrace we have been describing. Or add some other parental behaviors which produce the very opposite of meaningful touch and lasting commitment. Their consequences bring with them a "curse" rather than a "blessing."

• Alcoholism. There are between 12 to 15 million alcoholics in America. Every study of the adult children of alcoholics confirms they have serious problems with low self-esteem which results in an alarmingly high percentage of them either becoming alcoholics themselves or marrying alcoholics.

• Broken homes. By the early 1990s, one-half of all the children of our country will be from homes which have been broken by divorce. In January 1988 the U.S. Government reported that one-fourth of all children in the United States were living in single-parent homes.

• Latch-key kids. The latest Harris poll reports there are 13 million kids who go home from school every day to an empty house. This is one-fourth of all American homes. The same poll reported that teachers list this as the main reason why the children are not doing well in school (CBS Evening News, September 2, 1987).

• Abuse. It is almost impossible to keep up with the rising statistics on wife battering and the physical abuse of children. Reported cases of sexual abuse of children have doubled in less than a decade.

In many instances, it is mainly verbal abuse which is so damaging to the self-estimate. The Bible is right—as we think *in our hearts* so we are. Paul uses a remarkable phrase in Ephesians 1:18, *"the eyes of your heart."* Yes, our hearts do have *eyes* by which we see ourselves from the very depths of our personality. And when we see ourselves from the perspective of destructive *I am's,* then our self-esteem is affected from the very center of our being.

All of the factors we have been describing can produce self-devaluation and self-hate which may persist even after we have become Spirit-filled Christians, so that we then feel as if God too is disapproving of us. The first step in our healing is to realize that God understands where the feelings are coming from and is as brokenhearted about it as we are. He wants to work with us in freeing us from them, for He doesn't want His children despising themselves. Truly our only hope is a whole new way of viewing ourselves through the eyes of grace.

Seven times in the Gospel of John we find Christ's great I Am's: the bread of life (6:35), the light of the world (8:12), the door (10:7), the good shepherd (10:11), the resurrection and the life (11:25), the way, the truth, and the life (14:6), and the true vine (15:1). Jesus Christ was the only one who had the right to say, "I Am," because He is indeed the great I Am, incarnate in human flesh. It was Augustine who reminded us that you and I do not have the right to say "I am," because we never simply *are,* but are always in the process of *becoming.* What a wonderfully hopeful word! By God's grace we are becoming someone different. It's high time to leave the old "I am's" far behind.

I recently received a letter from a woman who, although a Christian for many years, had struggled with low self-esteem. She wrote, "Six simple words from your book transformed my life—'how much you mean to Him.'" I had thought only of how much He meant to me, so it never dawned on me that I could possibly mean anything to Him. When this really got through to me, it changed my whole feeling about myself!"

God is not like some cruel or neurotic parent, who needs to put down His children. On the contrary, He takes delight in lifting up His children and helping them feel good about themselves. "Consider the incredible love that the Father has shown us in allowing us to be called 'children of God'—and that is not just what we are called, but what we *are*" (1 John 3:1, PH). "Therefore, God is not ashamed to be called their God" (Hebrews 11:16).

It Takes an Inside Job

Our low self-worth will not be cured by something we may achieve or obtain from the outside. It has to come from the inside because the problem is so deep-rooted.

I have deliberately spent a lot of time on the destructive effects of dysgrace on self-image. Whatever its source— home, school, church, community, or culture—the consequences are a deep-rooted sense of worthlessness and self-despising. The common term we often use for this—*inferiority complex*—doesn't adequately describe the problem. When a person says, "I feel *inferior*," or "I feel *inadequate*," it's just another version of the old comparison game which puts the emphasis on *doing*. It often means inferior *to* someone because they *do it so much better*, or inadequate *for* a task. This sense of low self-esteem then is the result of not *doing* something well.

The sense of worthlessness and low self-esteem we are talking about is much more serious, because it involves a person's *being*. "I *am* worthless and unacceptable and the things I do just *reveal* to others what I really am. My failures and unacceptable behaviors simply *disclose* to people the kind of person I already know I am." Such people begin with what they think to *be an indisputable fact*—"I *am the kind of person no one could really like."* *What they do divulges who they feel they are.* No matter what successes they achieve, or how high they climb on the ladder, or how many compliments they receive from others, they still don't feel any better about themselves. The sense of being worthless and unacceptable comes first; the low self-esteem is already in their *being, and no amount of valuable, acceptable doing will change it.*

There's no other way to explain the fact that when others point out to them obviously successful accomplishments, or very acceptable and Christian behavior, it doesn't really get through to them. They hear it but can't believe or feel it at a gut level. Instead, they refuse to accept it and actually use it to add to their self-belittling in the most ingenious ways. Do any of these sound familiar?

People are just trying to make me feel good because they feel sorry for me.

I know it's not true and he's just stringing me along. I don't want that kind of pity.

My husband only tells me I look beautiful to make me feel better. I'd rather he'd tell me the truth (this one often from beautiful women).

My wife says she's proud of me, but it's just to make me feel good (this often from the most successful men).

People say that because they don't really know me.

You probably won't feel that way about me when you get to know me better.

I don't care how many compliments I get. When you begin with a zero, it doesn't make any difference what you add on; it's still a zero.

It really wasn't me who did it, it was the Lord (a common way self-effacing perfectionistic Christians fend off compliments, after they've done anything well, such as solos, sermons, services).

I appreciate what you're telling me, but after all you're my counselor! (Freely translated means, "I know you're trying to help, but you're not telling me the truth.")

Because this deep sense of low self-worth comes from within, it can never be solved by something outside of us. And yet we try. Let's look at a couple of the ways.

● The hunt for achievement. Many feel *if only* they could achieve success in some area of their work, they would prove themselves to be worthwhile. Then they would be accepted and loved by God and others, and therefore feel better about themselves. So they work harder, perform better, and may even achieve a high measure of success, only to discover that *no amount of doing or achieving* can change how they inwardly feel about themselves. Their low self-worth simply will not allow them to accept the appropriate affirmation and encouragement. So the whole vicious cycle starts all over again and the jaws of the performance trap grip them tighter than ever.

I would not want to generalize from my own experience, but it seems to me *more men* choose this route than do women. Men are more involved in their work and naturally think they can gain status and self-esteem *by their own efforts.*

● The hunger for affection. I see *more women* trying to gain a higher sense of self-worth through affection and love given them *by others.* Unfortunately, this is as unsatisfactory as the first. As several of the quoted personal putdowns indicated, their self-doubt will not allow them to accept the affection or love offered them. It's almost impossible for them to believe anyone could love them, when they consider themselves so undesirable, with little or nothing to offer in return. Once more a vicious circle is set up which varies from their being overanxious, overdemanding, overpossessive, or overcritical, all the way to being overaffectionate and sometimes even promiscuous. While there may be periods of temporary relief, such persons often cannot maintain the relationships for which they so desperately hunger.

Healing the Source

The primary sources of damage to our self-esteem need healing, repairing, and reprogramming. This is where healing grace is required. I want to make this as practical as possible, so let me make it personal and talk to you as if we were counseling together. Here are some of the questions I would ask.

• Have you found and faced the painful places in your past which you feel are the chief sources of your low self-esteem? It is very important that you have the courage not only to honestly look at the people and incidents involved, but also to plug into the feelings which go along with them. Brain research proves conclusively that our memories store not only mental pictures from the past *but also the original emotions experienced at that time.* So when you feel you have discovered the hurts, humiliations, deprivations, or rejections, allow yourself to *feel their pain and also to feel your reactions to that pain.* This not in order to *blame others* or to *escape responsibility.* It is done so that you can honestly face up to feelings you may have buried for years.

The best way to do this is *by sharing your feelings with God and with another person in prayer.* But you cannot confess to God what you will not first admit to yourself. When you also share with another person, this brings an even deeper level of openness and honesty with both yourself and God. This kind of openness can be very painful, and feelings may arise which will shock you. But grace is never shocked, never repulsed, and never withdrawn—whatever it is faced with. It is freely given, without any reference to our goodness or badness, worthiness or unworthiness.

The greatest manifestation of grace is the Cross, and the Cross means that when *God saw us at our worst, He loved us the most.* So armed with the courage grace can bring, look squarely at the worst, the most painful, the most humiliating, the most abusive, and the most devastating put-downs of your life. *Remember* them in your mind, and *relive* them in your emotions, but don't stop there. *Relinquish* them to God in forgiving and surrendering prayer. It's doubtful you can do this by yourself, so get help from a close friend, pastor, or counselor.

● As you have faced and felt the pain, have you forgiven everyone involved? As strange as it may sound, resentment and hate keep us chained to the people and the pains of the past. Only forgiveness and love can free us from both the painful memories and the destructive evaluations of the past. Sometimes this experience of healing grace comes about in unusual ways.

Arlene struggled with an extremely low opinion of herself. Though a really fine Christian who contributed to many areas of church life, she devalued her spiritual life. Much of our counseling had centered on her mother, a deeply religious woman, a leader in her denomination, but whose overcritical and perfectionistic ways had poured out as a constant stream over Arlene. As the hurts and humiliations surfaced, so did a heavy layer of resentment she had never faced. One day she was expressing it all so realistically I just presumed it was something which continued in present relationships with her mother. So I said to her, "It sure looks to me like you need to cut the umbilical cord to your mother, and stop letting her feed you with those downgrading evaluations." Arlene looked a bit startled. "Oh, I'm sorry," she said, "I guess I didn't make it plain. My mother's been dead for over five years now."

I was embarrassed and mumbled out an apology. I noticed Arlene clammed up for the rest of the session, so inwardly I was thinking, "Boy, Seamands, you sure blew it today!"

When she came back the next time she said to me, "I realize you know I'm a nurse, but do you know where I do most of my work?"

"No, I'm afraid I don't." I was still expecting some kind of scolding for last week's boner.

"Well, I spend most of my time in the labor room helping deliver babies. I suppose I've assisted doctors cut the umbilical cord hundreds of times. So last week when you said I needed to cut the umbilical cord to my mother, it really shocked me. As I drove home, the only thing I could picture in my mind was a cord 1,000 miles long stretching all the way from here right into my mother's grave down in Florida! I actually dreamed about that crazy cord twice. You were exactly right. This week I spent a lot of time in prayer, and I found the grace to forgive her, and to ask God to forgive me for resenting and blaming her all these years. And I've been amazed—I'm not feeding on her wretched evaluations of me anymore. I am beginning to get a whole new sense of *who I am as God's daughter, and I'm learning to feed on His opinions of me. And it's beginning to feel awfully good!*"

It would be impossible to exaggerate the importance of forgiveness in this regard. Forgiveness in the *active voice*—

forgiving those who have wronged and hurt us; in the *passive voice*—receiving forgiveness from God (and sometimes from others) for our wrong responses to their wrongs; and in the *reflective voice*—forgiving ourselves and refusing to continue flagellating ourselves for past sins.

The greatest barrier to receiving grace is an *unforgiving spirit.* This is especially true about the healing grace necessary to cure deep-rooted feelings of guilt, worthlessness, and self-hate. God has so created us that hidden resentments—even when we are not aware of them—create a kickback of guilt which creates a kickback of self-accusation and low self-esteem. Many times we cannot find freedom from this vicious circle because at some deep level we have not truly forgiven another.

Many people are unable to break out of this vicious circle by themselves, no matter how hard they try or how much they pray. If you are having difficulties in this area, surrender your pride and seek help from someone who can be for you a human "paraclete"—*someone called alongside to be a temporary assistant to the Holy Spirit.*

● Will you now commit yourself to daily cooperation with the Holy Spirit in giving you a new Christian self-image? Healing grace is not simply a one-time crisis gift. It may begin in a flash of insight or a very emotional high when we experience God's love and grace at a new and deeper level. *I would never belittle these spiritual highs in any way.* However, because emotions have been *badly overemphasized* in some Christian quarters, many pastors and counselors tend to *badly underemphasize* their importance. There are times when it takes a profoundly emotional experience to move a person off dead center, to loosen the mind from former mistaken perceptions, and *to actually free the will to make new decisions.* I have seen God work this way in many lives.

However, even when it *starts* that way, there is still the hard work of transformation by the renewal of the mind.

Old internal *put-down I am's* are hard to break. A daily, moment-by-moment cooperation with the *instant counter-activity of the Holy Spirit is essential.* When I recently had knee surgery, I learned that the operation was only *half of the healing.* Faithfully doing the exercises given me by the physical therapist *was the equally important other half.* The same is true in the therapeutic exercises following a dynamic experience of healing grace.

In my writings I have often quoted from the best-selling book, *Psycho-Cybernetics* by Dr. Maxwell Maltz. A former plastic surgeon, he turned to counseling because he discovered that unless people change their inner picture of themselves, it won't do much good to alter their appearance. Dr. Maltz's scientific research proved that it took about twenty-one days of inwardly repeating new ideas to effect permanent changes in people's views of themselves.

I find this a confirmation of the scriptural emphasis on putting off the old and putting on the new (Ephesians 4:22-24), and the exhortation to "think on such things" (Philippians 4:8). You may want to set a three-week period in which you listen to the Holy Spirit remind you of who you really are—your true *I am* and your *I am becoming.* Then think God's thoughts about you after Him. It will bring much joy to heaven and to you!

Eleven.
GRACE AND
NEGATIVE FEELINGS

Jesus, united by Thy grace,
And each to each endeared,
With confidence we seek Thy face,
And know our prayer is heard.

Help us to help each other, Lord,
Each other's cross to bear;
Let each his friendly aid afford,
And feel his brother's care.

P ressure is a key element of life in the performance trap. There is the pressure of trying to live with a self we don't like, a God who seems hard to love, and others we can't get along with. Put all together, it's the *pressure of feeling caught in a trap where we are expected to live up to unrealistic and impossible demands put upon us by God, ourselves, and other people.* And, like the hamster on the treadmill, the harder we try, the faster we run; and the faster we run, the harder we have to try to keep up with the wheel. This feeling of *being trapped* generates in us some strong negative emotions which keep us emotionally disturbed and spiritually defeated.

Anger and Depression
I have yet to counsel a performance-based and perfectionistic Christian who was not at heart *an angry person.* This doesn't mean such persons are always *aware of* or *express* it openly. They often impress us as being extremely controlled or very loving. But when we get to know them better, and they open up to share their inner selves, we inevitably discover a core of anger deep within their personalities.

However, the majority of those who come for help *are* conscious of the anger, because it is a major problem in their Christian lives. They struggle with resentments and sometimes even rage, and their seemingly uncontrollable outbursts of temper are the major factor in disrupting their personal relationships at work, in church, and especially with their spouses and children. They come across as angry persons, and angriest at themselves for being the way they are. This, of course, creates a vicious circle which increases their guilt, low self-esteem, and their sense of being phony—"What if people found out what I was really like when I blow up at my wife and kids?"

I find this unresolved anger, this frozen rage, to be the

chief source of the *depression* characteristic of the performance-bound person. No wonder many secular psychiatrists turn against religion when they see so many depressive patients who are scrupulous and overconscientious Christians. After all, if the ground of our right-relatedness to God is our own perfect performance, then we *ought* to be depressed and filled with feelings of angry hopelessness. For then we would truly be trapped in a no-win situation—*the ultimate injustice*—which would only add to our already existing vicious circle of negative emotions.

Thank God the ground of our relationship with Him is Christ's perfect performance for us—His perfect *life* of obedience and His perfect *death* for our sins. It is our faith in *Him,* our trusting receptivity of the gift of *His righteousness, in spite of all the sins and failures we see in ourselves,* which saves us from despair and depression. For the sake of those caught in the performance treadmill, let me assure you that this does not depend on a *perfect* repentance, or a *perfect* faith, or a *perfect* consecration on our part. George Whitefield used to say that even our *repentance* needs to be repented of. This is true about every ingredient involved in the human response to grace. Our *faith* itself needs to say to Jesus, "I do believe; help me overcome my unbelief!" (Mark 9:24) And *our surrender needs to be surrendered because it is not a perfect surrender.*

Let's look at some practical ways healing grace can deal with our anger and depression. As you read this, just imagine that you and I are talking together.

● Find and face the root sources of your anger and allow the grace of forgiveness to penetrate them. It is important that you discover who and what fill you with such anger and rage. It is not necessarily present-tense situations or persons who activate your anger. Rather, through them you are most likely tapping into the *core source* of your anger. Anger-filled persons are somewhat like telephone switchboards—through present events they plug into some past hurt and their whole system lights up. One way you can recognize this is *when your anger response is way out of proportion to the stimulus of the present situation.* Sometimes it's difficult to trace through the complex maze and find the true origin.

For both Gladys and her husband it was a second marriage. Their experiences were remarkably similar—their spouses had simply taken off with someone else and left the children with them. They had both lived as single parents for several years, had met in church, married, and now felt God had given them a wonderful second chance for a Christian family. They were very happy together and the children got along remarkably well. There was only one major problem. Gladys couldn't understand why her stepson, Mike, always seemed to rub her the wrong way. He was not a problem child and was affectionate and obedient to her. But Gladys had a strange sense of hostility toward him that resulted in her being harsh and overdemanding. Naturally it was beginning to affect the marriage and the whole family. She and her husband had communicated about it openly and she had spent many hours weeping and praying about it. We counseled together and prayed about it several times, but the mystery remained.

One day we talked about how her first husband, Ted, an alcoholic, had badly mistreated her. In the middle of the conversation she became silent. Sensing that the Great Counselor had taken over, I too kept quiet and inwardly prayed. After some time she began to express herself slowly, with long pauses in between, "I think I know what my problem is. . . . I never realized it before. . . . I see a great many of Ted's characteristics in Mike. . . . My goodness, he even looks something like him . . . has the same kind of build . . . and mannerisms. . . . I can't believe it. . . . He reminds me of him and that triggers off a lot of deeply buried hurts in me . . .

and I've just realized, I don't think I've fully forgiven Ted for what he did to me." Gladys began to cry softly, "You know, I've been taking out my feelings on Mike and he's completely innocent. No wonder we were *so confused by it all.*"

Now we knew *what we should be praying about.* It was a beautiful sight to see the forgiving, healing grace of the Cross cleanse away both the past source and the present stimulation for her anger. It was only a matter of time until they were enjoying a new level of loving relationships in the family.

Some good questions to ask are, *What am I really so angry about? Against whom am I actually so angry? Why does this (person/situation) make me so angry?* It's essential to face the primary roots of the problem and let grace deal with them. Hebrews 12:15 contains the heart of the matter in the form of a warning: "See to it that no one misses the grace of God and that no bitter root grows up to cause trouble and defile many." I have seen this bitter root grow in the lives of hundreds of Christians. They thought they were doing the right thing by not dwelling on the past, and so gave a kind of blanket forgiveness "to everyone who ever hurt me." And like a blanket, it covered but didn't really deal with the hurts and the hates. A bitter root was causing trouble and defiling a network of relationships. When the grace of God was applied like an axe at the root of the tree (Matthew 3:10), both the actual trouble and the diffusing defilement were taken care of.

● Face your explosive sense of injustice and allow the grace of acceptance to deactivate it. The performance-trapped and perfectionistic Christian usually feels a highly exaggerated sensitivity to anything unjust or unfair. It's like a ticking time bomb inside waiting to explode at the slightest contact with the inequities of life. Such persons often defend their angry oversensitivity by trying to turn it into a virtue. They have an insatiable need to set things right, to take up various *causes*, and to aggressively stand up for their rights. There is usually an unhealed wound in their past, where they were hurt or humiliated or treated unfairly, which feeds this heightened sense of injustice. Often these injustices reach all the way back into the early formative years of our lives.

Pip is the central figure of Charles Dickens' novel, *Great Expectations*, which many critics feel is his spiritual autobiography. One day after his cruel sister had humiliated him, Pip mused bitterly to himself:

My sister's bringing up had made me sensitive. In the little world in which children have their existence, whosoever brings them up, there is nothing so finely perceived and so finely felt as injustice. It may be only small injustice that the child can be exposed to; but the child is small, and its world is small, and its rocking-horse stands as many hands high, according to scale, as a big-boned Irish hunter. Within myself I had sustained, from my babyhood, a perpetual conflict with injustice. I had known, from the time when I could speak, that my sister, in her capricious and violent coercion, was unjust to me. Through all my punishments, disgraces, fasts and vigils, and other penitential performances, I had nursed this assurance.[1]

Too often, this nursed anger at injustice turns upward to be directed toward God; it is accompanied by a hidden resentment against Him. Such persons will often begin by saying they are angry at *life*. But when that is examined carefully, they realize the anger is actually against God. For as an old saying goes, "If you don't like the *design*, you don't like the *Designer*."

A dedicated Christian layman once said to me, "I've had to face the painful fact that for many years I've been angry with God. I've inwardly blamed Him for many things in my life which I felt were unfair. *I loved God, really did, I loved Him and served Him, but I didn't like Him!"* Much of this had to do with his failure to accept his personality type with his own gifts and talents. He had wasted many years "if-onlying," playing the comparison game, and angry at God because he wasn't more like a certain fellow-worker in the church. When he faced and relinquished his resentment against God, he learned not only to *accept* the personality gifts God had given him but also to *appreciate* them. Within a year God had begun to use him in a new way. People commented on the different expression on his face—less critical, more loving and caring. Slowly but surely he became a more winsome witness for Christ.

But this process involved considerable struggle, for at this point he was like all angry and depressed Christians. *They strongly feel they cannot pray—must not pray—they are too bad.* It seems as if God is disappointed and angry with them. They have lost the sense of God as loving and personal, fatherly and friendly, giving and gracious. From their emotional pit they perceive God not as the giver of unconditional love, but as one who bargains before He blesses. So while they keep on working—perhaps even harder, they stop praying in any deep sense of the word. They feel they cannot share their true selves with God, not when they have such anxiety, conflict, and depression. If they do pray, their prayers are perfunctory and unreal.

If you are caught in this kind of a trap, I have good news for you. Your hope is in looking to the Cross. There the Incarnate God voluntarily took upon Himself all the sins, the meaningless suffering, the unmerited pain and undeserved injustices of the world. There He bore all that the whole world—including *you and I*—could angrily heap upon Him. So He is not shocked by anything we may now express to Him out of our inner emotional pain and suffering. Again and again I have seen the miracle of healing grace penetrate and defuse anger, rage, and depression *when people resume talking to God in prayer.* Often those prayers begin with, "O God, it's been a long time since I've been able to talk to You. I felt I couldn't with all my feelings about You. . . ." After the sound barrier is broken and communication is reestablished, healing grace begins to penetrate those negative emotions. Ultimately they experience an inflow of the love of God on a deeper level than ever before. Often this healing takes place with the help of other humans who understand and accept us *as we are*—friends, pastors, counselors, or a small group.

But the most wonderful part of all is that *God Himself lovingly works with us* to heal our hurts, defuse our hypersensitivity to injustice, and change us from *fighters into lovers, defenders into reconcilers.* His healing grace removes barriers which for so long have kept us from experiencing His sanctifying grace in our lives. We do not need to hesitate in the least to express in prayer our anger and depression, *even when it is against Him.* He has known about it long before we confess it to Him, and has continued to love us. Indeed, it is *His very grace* faithfully working in us which now enables us to both *own it and then to disown it.*

Fears and Compulsions

Some people are subject to strange and irrational fears, panic attacks, obsessive thoughts or ideas, and uncontrollable compulsions. Persons troubled by these symptoms are usually very high-strung, nervous, supersensitive, and with family tendencies toward alcoholism, depression, and emotional breakdown.

If you are identifying with this description, my first word of grace is to caution you against *assuming such prob-*

lems always have a spiritual cause. In recent years much research has been done which reveals that there are often neurological or chemical causes behind such symptoms. It is strange we evangelical Christians have no qualms about taking medicine or shots for diabetes, thyroid problems, or high blood pressure. But when it comes to matters of depression, panic attacks, and the like, we assume we must solve them *only by spiritual means.* Indeed, this in itself contributes to our unrealistic ideals and unreachable goals—"If I were really spiritual, then I would be able to handle this."

Before making such assaults on yourself, *check with a physician about any possible medical causes which may require treatment or medication.* And don't allow your superspiritual Christian friends to put a guilt trip on you for getting this kind of help. It's hard for us to imagine, but when anesthesia was first discovered, vast numbers of preachers thundered against it. Nowadays when we have to undergo an operation, we thank God for it. Remember, God made *all* the elements of this universe; if medication helps you live a better Christian life, then receive it too *as a gift of His grace.* Of course, this can be overdone; but the answer to *misuse* is not *disuse,* but *right use.*

Imbalanced chemistry, inadequate theology, and insufficient grace are very able to work together to exacerbate the performance/perfectionist trap. Each one feeds the other, making it difficult to know where one begins and other ends. For we know that mental patterns and spiritual outlook influence our body chemistry. *There is no more powerful medicine than grace and love.* A gut-level experience of being unconditionally accepted, forgiven, loved—God's grace—can bring about incredible miracles of change.

Pauline, a pastor's wife in her early thirties, came seeking help with the whole pattern of problems we have been describing. She had had recurring bouts with anxiety attacks since her teen years. She had a long history of being overloaded with Christian role-expectations which she felt she had to live up to. The panic attacks, lasting for a few hours or several days, terrified her, and always left her physically exhausted and deeply depressed. Within her extended family, there was alcoholism, emotional breakdown, and some traumatic deaths. Ordinarily she could control her fears, but when a panic attack struck, she was overwhelmed by the thought, "Will it happen to me?" When this happened she was unable to sleep properly; then she would feel terribly guilty because she was not trusting God. It was a no-win situation.

We worked together for many hours on the terrible pressure her superspiritual self put on her. She read and reread books on grace and we spent time praying together. She would often say, *"Grace is so hard. It's so hard to let God love me.* I've been a Christian since I was twelve, but I've never really believed God loved me, the real me." Together we traced the roots of this, not just to an unpredictable, unaffectionate, and graceless home, but also to a pastor who was one of God's strict and stoical servants. She shared numberless injustices and hurt, and shed many angry tears. These were always followed by, "I'm so ashamed for you to see me *this way."* Finally, with the barriers removed, grace broke through to the real Pauline. This is how she described it when I asked her to write it down for me.

> I remember I didn't feel very much like going to my session with Dr. Seamands that morning. I was very tired. Both of the children were just getting over the chicken pox and I had slept very little the nights before. But maybe that's how it is, God can really work when we're weak, tired, and completely dependent on Him. After sharing with him I started to go down the stairs, although previously I always took the

elevator. It was on that walk down the stairs God started to speak to me in a special way.

"Thank You, God, for breaking through," were the words which ran in my heart over and over again. Slowly the tears started coming, and when I got to the car the dam broke. I sat there and cried and cried as I let God reveal Himself to me, as I let Him minister to me. . . . Yes, His love was finally breaking through. I was experiencing His love as never before. In my mind, I saw Jesus with the children on His lap and I, as a child, was walking toward Him. "I want to climb on Your lap and be loved by You," were my thoughts. I was approaching Him and the disciples were scaring me away with, "He's too busy, too tired, go away." But Jesus stretched out His arms to me . . . Dare I enter His embrace? . . . Oh yes, I'll let Him love me and liberate me.

Nothing else matters anymore except God's love. He really loves me! His love penetrates, permeates my very being. Thank You, God! My heart is filled with such joy and peace. How wonderful to feel Your love. "Release me, God, from my own self-made, self-imposed prison constructed by my own wrong concepts of You. . . . "

The thought often comes to me now, that as I love my own son always, *even when he's bad* . . . I say to him, "Mommy loves you always; you don't have to be good for Mommy to love you." And that's what I hear God saying to me, "Pauline, you don't have to be good in order for Me to love you." Thank You, God, for finally breaking through. . . .

This was how grace came through to Pauline. It was the beginning of new freedom and a new physical and spiritual health. She continues to minister to others out of a grateful and grace-filled heart. Don't be misled by the dramatic crisis experience she described. That was made possible because of a long process which removed her inner barriers to grace—some of which went right back to her childhood years. How tender and beautiful of the Spirit to enable her to become a participant in the Gospel story of Jesus and the children. This brought the necessary healing from the wounds of deprivation and rejection so that she could accept God's grace. I firmly believe there is a tailor-made experience of healing grace for you too, if, like Pauline, you will *let God love you just as you are.*

Group Grace

Let me now address one of the most important but badly neglected aspects of healing grace. Many of the worst barriers to God's grace come from the dysgrace of unhealthy and destructive personal relationships in our past. Therefore many of those barriers will *be removed largely through healthy and constructive personal relationships in our present.* This is where *group grace* enters the picture.

At the very heart of the great healing passage in James 5:13-20 are these words, "Therefore confess your sins to each other and pray for each other so that you may be healed" (v. 16). Some wit has commented that many Christians and church groups have reversed that advice—they confess sins *for* each other and then pray *at* one another! In the early church, *koinonia*—a sharing, giving fellowship—was placed on a par with doctrine, prayer, worship, and the Lord's Supper (Acts 2:42). Since they did not have church buildings, they met mostly in small group gatherings in homes and other convenient places. Very open sharing and confession was made to the group which then supported the struggling person with their love and prayers. Not until the third century did the practice of private confession begin which finally resulted in the "sealing of the confessional," turning it into a strictly private matter. Thus, with a few rare exceptions, the healing power of group grace was largely lost to the church.

It was rediscovered on a large scale during the great Evangelical Revival in Britain under the Wesleys. The Methodist Church did not begin as a church but as associations of like-minded people or "societies." These were small groups of five to ten persons, led by converted laypersons, and meeting weekly in "class meetings" to study Scripture, share, and pray together. Church historians give full credit to the Spirit-anointed preaching of George Whitefield and John Wesley, and the inspiring hymns of Charles Wesley, for generating the revival. But all agree *it was the incredible power of these small groups which brought about such lasting transformation in individuals and ultimately "spread Scriptural holiness and reformed the nation."*

Unfortunately, most churches today have overlooked this great potential for changing lives, and organizations like Alcoholics Anonymous have taken it up. AA's roots can be traced back through the Oxford Movement to those early Methodist Societies. AA was founded by the famous Bill W., an alcoholic whose life had been changed through the sharing and prayer of the group meetings in an Episcopal Church. While some AA chapters today have gotten away from their Christian roots, they still use the group principles with great effectiveness.

Early in this book we described one of the saddest and costliest consequences of performance-oriented living—a sense of feeling phony, duplicitous, and alienated from our real selves. This is because such Christians let people know only their superselves. They present a *public self* to others because this is the concept of themselves they want people to believe. Actually, there are assorted *public selves presented to different people.* In this way they become so estranged from their *private self* they no longer know who and what they really are. This is one of their major sources of self-despising and inner anxiety. It keeps them feeling like hypocrites and drains their power for living and for witnessing.

Persons who live this way have literally sold their souls, their true selves, in order to gain the approval, affection, or acclaim of others. And the longer they are on the performance treadmill, the more fearful and secretive they tend to become. The only way they can get off this destructive wheel is to allow others to know their *real selves*. We all remember Socrates' famous dictum, "Know thyself." I believe the truth can better be expressed, "Let thyself be known and thou wilt know thyself."

We talk a lot about being honest with ourselves and with God. And we sincerely—sometimes desperately—try to do this in our times of Bible reading and prayer. But the kind of honesty and self-knowledge which will bring about lasting changes in our lives *almost always requires another person. It is when we disclose our true, private selves to someone else that we fully come to know ourselves for real.* Down deep we may dimly perceive the truth about our *real selves*, yet go on denying or covering it with our superselves— even in prayer. However, once we have actually put the truth into words and shared with another, it becomes increasingly difficult to continue deceiving ourselves.

Yes, it is the truth that sets us free—the truth about God and ourselves which Christ alone brings to us (John 8:32-36). And a major part of that truth about ourselves is communicated when, at cost to our false superselves, we allow others to know the truth about us. And this is where the Body Life of the Church becomes the channel of grace. It surrounds us with the trust atmosphere of our new Family of God which gives us the courage to be truly known by our brothers and sisters in Christ. Not only *known* but *loved!* This frees us from having to be someone and something we are not, since we are *accepted and loved as we are.* In this way we discover the life-transforming power of group grace.

Performance-minded and perfectionistic Christians especially need such an accepting and loving fellowship *where they can disclose their real selves without fear of disapproval and condemnation.* Trying to get out of the performance trap by *only* their own *individual* struggle is as impossible as climbing out of quicksand without a helping hand. James 5:16 infers there are some physical, emotional, and spiritual hangups which can *only* be healed when they are shared with and prayed for by other Christians.

This may begin with just one other person—a trustworthy friend, Sunday School teacher, pastor, or counselor. And there are some things which should be shared only in that confidential setting. However, *there are many of us who as soon as possible need to share and pray with a small group. There is an amazing and life-transforming power in this kind of group grace.* If you cannot find such a group, then find at least one other person—perhaps through your contacts in a Sunday School class—and *start a group by opening your life to that person.* Then let it spread to include another and another. You can usually find someone who is desperately looking for such fellowship. This transparent openness and agreed praying (Matthew 18:18-20) sets off a kind of spiritual nuclear fission which generates great power. It will explode and disintegrate those obstacles to grace in your life and allow God to set you free to live and love in the Spirit.

Recycling Grace

The ultimate purpose of grace is to prepare us for fellowship with God throughout eternity, so that we can truly worship Him and literally "enjoy Him forever." But what is the ultimate purpose of healing grace as far as our lives here on earth are concerned? It is more than salvation, sanctification, or even restoration to wholeness. His ultimate design is to take everything that has ever happened in our lives and turn it to God's purposes for good. Everything? Some of you are thinking of some unspeakably evil and painful things which either *you, or someone else, meant for evil.* Things which have left you damaged and crippled in some way—physically, mentally, emotionally, spiritually, or relationally. Some wrongs which could only be called *garbage.* Is God able to even use such things as grist for His mill and turn them for human good and His glory?

And with all the strength within me I want to say an unqualified YES! If we humans are able to build plants which can recycle garbage into usable fuel, then certainly God can do the same. The most exciting part of my ministry has been watching God do this in the lives of those who have experienced His healing grace. These people are literally the *wounded healers and the healed helpers.* God has been able to take their very *cripplings* and turn them into *blessings.*

In my mind I see a veritable parade of people, literally a "cloud of witnesses," who have experienced every kind of personal sin, evil, victimization, dysgrace, and damaged emotion you could possibly imagine. But they all experienced God's healing grace at a deep level. *Now they are ministering to other hurting people out of the very places where they were hurt the most.*

I'm thinking of several Christian young men who came seeking help for their struggles with homosexuality. There were hours of counseling, prayers for healing, and a long time of reprogramming which included accountability and encouragement from a small support group. They are now happily married, with families, and God has given them a special ministry to others with the same problem.

I am also remembering a large number of disheartened Christians with varying degrees of perfectionism. Legalistic, critical, and judgmental, imprisoned by worry and worthlessness, believing wrong concepts of God, and driven to find approval from God and others. Many came for help when their tightly woven system began to come apart at the seams. Some came during or just after an emotional and spiritual breakdown. Some had to be hospitalized under psychiatric care. No, there were no quick cures; it was often a lengthy, uphill struggle against well-entrenched patterns of performance-based living. But ultimately grace broke through and they became resting believers instead of restive achievers. I have likened them to persons thrashing around in the water because they felt as if they were drowning. And then finally being saved when they began believing and living out grace—*they stopped their futile efforts and trusted the water to hold them up.* Now they are expert swimmers and have a special ministry to the performance-trapped. Because they understand and know how to suffer with their struggles, God is using them to bring freedom to the imprisoned.

And then I think of all those who were victims of sexual abuse, including what is perhaps the most destructive of all, incest. In *Putting Away Childish Things*, I shared the testimony of one such victim, her remarkable healing, and how God allowed her to lead her dying father to Christ. God has used this woman in a remarkable ministry to other incest victims.

I stress all this because there are simply not enough professionally trained counselors to work with the growing numbers of damaged and hurting people. God wants to raise up a vast army of healed helpers whom He can use as His "temporary assistants to the Holy Spirit." This is the ultimate purpose of healing grace in your life—to turn you into a channel of healing grace in someone else's life. Let me share a letter from one young man God is using in this way.

I want to remind you of the first line of my journal entry a year ago today. This was about a week before you took me to the airport to send me home. 'I am at the lowest point in my life. I feel like a total failure.'

I find it hard to believe that God could change me so drastically in one year's time. This time last year I was filled with self-hatred, hopelessness, and despair. Today I can honestly say that I like myself; the future has never seemed brighter. My life is filled to overflowing with peace and joy. God's grace is my watchword. He fills up whatever is lacking in me with His grace. He is a faithful God! I know this is a permanent condition for me. I've been like this for about six months now.

This afternoon I prayed with a young man who received Christ in his heart. And tonight I shared my walk with the Lord (depression, sins, failures, and all) with a young lady to help strengthen her newfound faith in Jesus. We both got excited. God is such a faithful God. I'm just basking in His grace!

Twelve.

THE PANORAMA
OF GOD'S GRACE

What shall I do my God to love,
My loving God to praise!
The length, and breadth, and height to prove,
And depth of sovereign grace.

Thy sovereign grace to all extends,
Immense and unconfined;
From age to age it never ends,
It reaches all mankind.

Throughout the world its breadth is known,
Wide as infinity,
So wide it never passed by one;
Or it had passed by me.

To restrict God's grace only to saving or sanctifying grace would be to miss the all-encompassing nature of God's love in action. It would be like looking at the spectacular beauty of the Matterhorn and thinking you had seen the Alps; or showing people a picture of awesome Mount Everest and telling them it was the Himalayas. Both of these peaks are outstanding for their beauty and height, but they are surrounded by a breathtaking range of mountains which serve to highlight their grandeur.

And so it is with the grace of God. Certainly there are mountain-peak experiences, but grace includes a wide diversity of "mysterious ways" in which God works "His wonders to perform." Let us look at some of the levels of the grace God reaches out toward us.

General Grace

Many sincere evangelical Christians today are running scared. They want to be truly biblical and to avoid all attempts to dilute or corrupt the Christian faith. Unfortunately, they have gone to the opposite extreme and forgotten a very important teaching of Scripture itself, that "every good and perfect gift is from above, coming down from the Father" (James 1:17). The greatest Christian thinkers and teachers, from the early church fathers through Augustine, Luther, Calvin, and Wesley, have taught that *everything* true, good, beautiful, and helpful in this world is actually a gift of God, *regardless of where it came from or how it got here.* They used many different terms for this idea, but they all linked it to God's compassion and grace for the whole world.

On the simplest level, there are the everyday gifts we all take for granted, which preserve life on this earth. "Your Father in heaven," said Jesus, "causes His sun to rise on the evil and the good, and sends rain on the righteous and the unrighteous" (Matthew 5:45). "The Lord is gracious and compassionate, slow to anger and rich in love. The Lord is good to all; He has compassion on all He has made" (Psalm 145:8-9).

On a higher level, some of the basics of human nature such as conscience, reason, and the ability to think and discover truth are gifts from God. Paul uses this idea to hold everyone responsible before God (Romans 1:19-20; 2:12-15). Of course, this *discovered truth* is not on the same level as *God's revealed truth*. *It cannot save us, but it is truth just the same, and has come from God.*

I get a lot of letters and calls from sincere Christians who say something like this, "Thanks for your books; they've helped me a lot. But I don't understand; it sounds like you believe in *psychology.*" I always reply, "Of course I do, and I believe in *sociology, criminology, urology, radiology, political science, mathematics, computer science, aerodynamics,* and *scores of other sources of knowledge, because I believe God is the source of all truth.*" It's just my way of trying to get them to appreciate all of God's gracious gifts, even those that might come to us through unusual channels.

The great reformer and theologian, John Calvin, wrote much about the positive merit of man's "terrestrial" culture which includes all "civil polity, domestic economy, all the mechanical arts and liberal sciences." He even referred to heathen writers, philosophers, and poets by saying,

> If we believe that the Spirit of God is the only fountain of truth, we shall neither reject nor despise the truth itself, wherever it shall appear, unless we wish to insult the Spirit of God. . . . All truth is from God, and consequently if wicked men have said anything that is true and just, we ought not to reject it, for it has come from God."[1]

What Calvin called "common grace," John Wesley included within "prevenient grace," crediting God as the author of all wisdom and understanding in mankind. But all of them really go back to Augustine, who coined the phrase, "plundering the Egyptians." This meant we Christians have a right to take the truth wherever and however God gives it to us.

The most amazing example of this is in the Bible itself. When Paul was preaching at Athens he quoted non-Christian philosophers and poets in his sermon. How many times we have all heard someone refer to those beautiful words of Scripture, "In Him we live and move and have our being" (Acts 17:28). We don't stop to realize that Paul is quoting a pagan philosopher of his day!

Why do we stress this primary and generalized idea of grace? So that we will be open to let God speak to us in any way He chooses. We do not need to be afraid of anything helpful which comes through these channels. Because God has given us the special revelation of Himself in His Word, we can test everything by Scripture. That does *not* mean we will necessarily find it in the Bible in the words we use today. Rather, our concern should be whether an idea agrees with the principles of Scripture. Anything that meets *this test* we can receive *with gratitude to God.*

Many people ask me, "Where in the Bible does it talk about inner healing or the healing of memories?" I usually reply, "It's in the same chapter which said it was okay for my daughter to have an emergency appendectomy which saved her life!"

Yes, we are thankful for each new truth, insight, invention, or discovery which comes to us from such fields as medicine, psychology, sociology, and any other branches of human knowledge. Of course, there are evil people who can use them for sinful purposes. The same airplane that carries missionaries to reach people with the Gospel can be used to drop bombs and kill them. *The answer to misuse is not disuse.* As Christians, we are *required* by God to use every gift He has given us for His glory and for human good.

Restraining Grace

If God had abandoned the creation and His creatures after the Fall by allowing the consequences of sin to have their full effects, the human race would have never survived. His love and compassion is shown in many forms of what has been called restraining grace.

Though sin has badly damaged our power of reason, God did not allow it to be destroyed. So even unsaved and unregenerate humans have this amazing gift from God—a mind which can reason, think, remember, imagine, discover, and invent. Far above and beyond all other creatures, we humans can understand the relationship between cause and effect. No, we cannot by reasoning find God or work out our own salvation. We don't even have the power to live up to the best we can reason. But God has worked through the gift of reason to help hold sin in check.

The Bible suggests that human governments which make and enforce laws are God's agents in restraining the power of evil in the world. Paul states this clearly in Romans 13:1-7 where he points out that a human ruler is "God's servant to do you good. But if you do wrong be afraid . . . for he is God's servant, an agent of wrath to bring punishment on the wrongdoer" (v. 4). Peter writes in a similar way in his first epistle (2:13-14). I remind you that they are both writing about a system we Americans would consider cruel and at times evil—the Roman Empire. But they still considered it "an agent of God" for good. I used to wonder about this until I had a most unusual missionary experience.

India became an independent nation in 1947. All of the native states joined the new government except Hyderabad State, the one in which we lived. India tried to settle the issue by every possible peaceful and diplomatic measure, but to no avail. Finally in 1948, the Indian government sent in its army and took over by force. But they were a bit too successful and captured our town a day ahead of schedule. The army then camped outside the city and waited for the new civil administration team. However, they didn't arrive until the next day. So we lived in a town of 35,000 people for 24 hours *without any government.* That night stores and houses were robbed and burned. In those days food was rationed, and the central warehouse housing the grain was looted. *I saw human nature without the restraints of enforced law and order,* and it is a sight I hope never to see again. I learned that some government, though bad, is better than no government. The country or the culture makes no difference, for exactly the same things happened during the terrible riots of the '60s in Detroit, Chicago, and Los Angeles. I now understand what those Scriptures mean and how important God's restraining grace is. Did we ever stop to thank God for His restraining grace which was at work in our lives *long before we came to know Him as our Saviour?* His restraining grace not only held us back from deeper sin, it also prevented us from being the victims of even worse evil. One of the stanzas of the hymn, "Now the Day Is Over," expresses this so beautifully.

> Comfort every sufferer
> Watching late in pain;
> Those who plan some evil,
> From their sins restrain.

In his excellent book, *The Way,*[2] Dr. E. Stanley Jones states that the earliest name for Christians was "those who belonged to the Way" (Acts 9:2; 19:23; 24:22). Of course, this refers to the way of salvation, but Dr. Jones enlarges it to also mean God's Way, the right way for everything— the way to think, feel, and act. It is the Way God has written into the nature of everything in the universe, so that life sifts down to two basic alternatives, the Way and not the Way. And the Christian way is always the right way and the unchristian way is always the wrong way.

Why is this? Because God has superimposed external laws upon us, like the Ten Commandments? No, because God has woven those laws into the fabric of the entire universe. The Way is something given; we don't produce it, we don't build it; it's just there in the nature of things. And we must come to terms with this Way and its principles, or get hurt. Thus we do not break these laws written into the nature of things; we only break ourselves on them. When we fall from a tall building, we don't *break* the law of gravity; we only *demonstrate* it when we hit the ground. And these built-in laws are manifestations of God's preventive grace; they are barriers put up at the edge of the precipice to keep us from going over. Jones quoted a surgeon who confirmed this principle. "I've discovered the kingdom of God at the end of my scalpel. It's in the tissues. The right thing morally is always the healthy thing physically."

I have used Dr. Jones' idea in my counseling ministry for many years, pointing out to people how the universe either works for us or against us. I remember a married woman who shared with me her infatuation for another man and her strong temptation to have an affair with him. She was a Christian and the Holy Spirit had been faithful in checking her impulses. But now she was beginning to rationalize and I could see it was probably only a matter of time until she yielded. Of course, she knew the biblical commandments against this, but they didn't seem to be enough to deter her. I was trying to get her to see how

God's built-in moral laws operate in all our interpersonal relationships, and that the affair was doomed to futility and frustration. I kept explaining, "You can choose to go ahead with this, but the universe won't back you. You are going against it and it will go against you." After awhile she began to give in to the temptation and started down the slippery slope toward a full-blown affair. Thank God, before that took place she found herself on the verge of physical and emotional breakdown. When she came back to see me she said, "I didn't believe you when you told me, 'The universe won't back you in this.' But you were right. All sorts of things have happened to trouble me—in my body, my mind, my emotions, and my interpersonal family relationships."

She discovered what E. Stanley Jones wrote nearly a half-century before. "The word *evil* is the word *live* spelled backwards. It is life attempting to live against itself. And that can't be done . . . it is an attempt to live against the nature of reality and get away with it. It is an attempt at the impossible. The result is inevitable—breakdown and frustration."³ This incident reminded me of an ancient proverb said to be quoted by sailors, "He who spits against the wind spits in his own face."

The Apostle Paul is the perfect scriptural illustration of this form of grace. While he was still called Saul, he was confronted by the risen Christ on the road to Damascus, "Saul, Saul, why do you persecute Me? It is hard for you to kick against the goads" (Acts 26:14). Jesus was using a common picture from ancient life. When a young ox was first yoked, it would try to kick its way out. But in doing so it only hurt itself more on a jagged spike, the goad, placed there for this very purpose. The more it kicked against the goads, the sharper the pain. It was the goads which brought it into submission. Unfortunately, we too often have to learn the hard way, and God has built His goads of grace into all of life. First Peter 3:12 is a quote from Psalm 34:16: "The face of the Lord is against those who do evil." This "againstness" toward wrong has been written into all of life. When we understand this, we see God's anger in a completely different light. We discover God's judgment is actually a form of His mercy. We understand it as the opposite side of the coin of His love manifested in His restraining grace. It is one of the gracious ways God uses to turn us away from sin and toward Himself, in order to redeem and restore us.

Seeking Grace

Finally we come to the grace of God which seeks us for our salvation. Of course, throughout all of the various kinds of grace we have been saying God's central purpose is to bring us all to the place of repentance, faith, and new life in Christ. "He is patient with you, not wanting anyone to perish, but everyone to come to repentance" (2 Peter 3:9). So this is God's design woven into the total fabric of life. But there comes the time when we can actually sense His seeking grace at work in more specific ways.

Many of us forget that back of the familiar "We love Him because He first loved us" (1 John 4:19, KJV) is an even prior truth. We *seek* Him because He *first sought us.* Theologians throughout the ages have realized that one of the chief ways God seeks us is by creating within us a hunger to seek Him. Even we Christians, since we are human beings, tend to overlook this and become self-centered in our testimonies. John tells us in his Gospel (1:43) that "Jesus decided to leave for Galilee. Finding Philip He said to him, 'Follow Me.' " Then two verses later (1:45) he says, "Philip found Nathaniel and told him, 'We have found the One Moses wrote about . . . Jesus of Nazareth.' " What an interesting contrast. Philip claims he "found Jesus." Actually prior to this Jesus had found him! Prodding grace means God is always first on the scene long before we even think about Him. An unknown hymn writer says it best.

I sought the Lord and afterward I knew
He moved my soul to seek Him, seeking me.
It was not I that found, O Saviour true,
No, I was found of Thee.

Thou didst reach forth Thy hand and mine enfold,
I walked and sank not on the storm-vexed sea;
'Twas not so much that I on Thee took hold
As Thou, dear Lord, on me.

I find, I walk, I love, But oh, the whole of love
Is but my answer, Lord, to Thee!
For Thou wert long beforehand with my soul;
Always Thou lovedst me."[4]

We must always remember when we talk about "seeking God," or "searching for truth," or "following after light," the only reason we do any of those things is because God is already at work in our hearts prodding us with His seeking grace.

While I was preaching a Spiritual Life series at a university, a young man named Jack came to counsel with me. Like many other preachers' kids, he was rebelling against the faith of his parents and his own preteen conversion experience. He told me his story with deep shame. In his attempt to run from God he had deliberately dated a girl well known on campus for her loose morals. They had faked a signout to go to their homes for the weekend but ended up in a distant motel, spending the night together. However, what he had fantasized as a night of ecstatic pleasure turned out to be quite different. Now he felt guilty, empty and, worst of all, abandoned by God. He kept saying to me, "I just can't seem to find Him again." I kept answering, "What you really mean, Jack, is you can't get away from Him." He asked me to explain what I had said, for it was the opposite of what he felt. I opened my Bible to Psalm 139:7-8, handed it to him, and asked him to read it. He began reading as it is found in the *King James Version*. "Whither shall I go from Thy Spirit? or whither shall I flee from Thy presence? If I ascend up into heaven, Thou art there; if I make my bed. . . ." He stopped. I said, "Go on, Jack, finish it." He continued slowly, "If I make my bed in hell, behold Thou art there." I asked, "Jack, who do you think you met in that motel room?" He looked puzzled. "I don't understand. Do you mean the . . . the girl?" I replied, "No, no, Jack. I mean *God*. Don't you realize when you tried to run *from* God, you ran right smack *into* Him that night in the motel? In fact God was never nearer than then." Big tears began to trickle down his cheeks. Soon we were praying to the One who had never stopped seeking His wayward son. God's *love* had never changed, only His *strategy*. Jack learned you can *refuse* God's love, but you can't *lose* it when the Hound of Heaven is on your trail!

Sometimes God *seeks us by letting us go. Letting us go our own way and allowing us to suffer the inevitable consequences of that way in the hope that our suffering will bring us back to Him.*

In the greatest seeking chapter of Scripture, Luke 15, we see this so clearly. In the case of the Lost Sheep and the Lost Coin, there is direct action until the lost is found. But in the case of the Lost Boy (the Prodigal Son), this is not the case. The Father is silent—he does not *speak to him.* He seems inactive—he does not *stop him.* He does not *seek him* by going after him. He *seeks him by keeping quiet and letting him go into a distant country where someday a "severe famine" will occur, and he will "begin to be in need,"* and perhaps he will come *"to his senses."*

Back in the early '70s, a young man named Andy came for help. He had reached the end of his rope, was in a deep depression, and had been contemplating suicide. As I sat and listened to his story I couldn't help thinking of Jesus' Parable of the Prodigal. In my mind I followed the parallel at every step. Andy had run away from a good home, gotten into heavy drugs, and begun to lose control of his drinking. Prior to his enrollment at Asbury College he had been living in a commune in an eastern city. The three fellows and two girls shared everything—lodging, food, and sex. But life had fallen apart. Now he was empty and fed up.

Before I realized what I was saying I blurted out, "You know, Andy, you've done everything the Prodigal did except eat the pigs' food." He looked startled and fell silent. I started to apologize, thinking I'd said the wrong thing, but the Holy Spirit was way ahead of me.

"Oh no," he said, "I just remembered . . . I've even done that!"

Now it was my turn to look startled. "What in the world do you mean?"

"Well, I attended the great Woodstock Rock Festival in '69. You remember the crowd was so huge (over 400,000) they ran out of food, and we ended up almost starving. But no one could get out to buy food. So finally helicopters flew over and dropped macrobiotic hog food in huge bundles. And we all grabbed it and ate it with our bare hands." Andy groaned out a disgusting "Yuk" as he remembered the taste.

After that there was only one incident of the parable left for Andy to make the parallel complete—the journey back to the Father's house. Before long that part of the story had also been fulfilled! Thank God for His steadfast love and His faithful grace which reaches into every human situation. God sometimes does this by allowing sin and evil to overplay its hand. He permits it to go too far until there is a kickback of consequences. And God takes this opportunity to woo us and win us through painful grace.

Saving Grace

Finally, there is the direct action of the seeking Spirit of God upon the human spirit. At this point *all of the influences of the previous forms of grace are gathered together and the pressure of the immediate presence of God is evident in the consciousness of the person.* This is the supreme moment in the divine-human encounter. "Here I am!" says Jesus, in Revelation 3:20. "I stand at the door and knock. If anyone hears My voice and opens the door, I will go in and eat with him, and he with Me." The Holy Spirit of God is on the outside knocking and speaking. He is also within us, opening our ears so we can hear and giving us the will and the ability to respond. It is He who offers us the gift of faith so we can trust in spite of all our fears and hesitations. It is all of God's grace. Even the "faith" is "not from (y)ourselves, it is the gift of God" (Ephesians 2:8).

A great example of the pursuing grace of God is given us by John Bunyan, the author of *Pilgrim's Progress.* In another one of his writings, *Grace Abounding,* he tells of the time in his life when he was running from God. Bunyan calls these times his "flying fits." He says during those moments, when he literally fled from God, a certain verse from the Book of Isaiah would continuously come to his mind. It was so vivid and real to his memory it was as if the passage actually called out after him. "I have blotted out as a thick cloud thy transgressions, and as a cloud thy sins. Return unto Me, for I have redeemed you" (Isaiah 44:22). He writes, "This would make me stop for a while, and, as it were, look over my shoulder behind me to see if I could discern that the *God of grace would follow me with a pardon in His hand.''* What a striking picture of the pursuing grace of a loving God. Let us not think that this kind of direct initiative by God's Spirit is limited to times past. Again and again I have been astounded by it. I was when a lady shared her story with me.

Linda is now a pastor's wife, and a radiant, Spirit-filled Christian. But she did not come from that kind of back-ground—quite the opposite. She was a battered child, abused physically and sexually by her own brothers and a stepfather. This had filled her with deep shame and low self-esteem which had plunged her deeper into sin. Finally she ran away from home and ended up at eighteen years of age in New York City. She was alone and had very few friends. One night, literally in a den of evil, she was sitting on a chair in a room. She was practically naked, and in the same room on the bed was a couple engaged in sexual intercourse. There swept over her a devastating sense of loneliness and guilt. The terrible realization of *where* she was and *who* she was and the fact *no one really cared* overwhelmed her. She suddenly realized the utter selfishness of the scene—everyone there was using each other and using her. It hit her like a thunderbolt and filled her with awful blackness, depression, and despair.

But in the midst of that situation there came (what she called) an overshadowing sense of the presence of God. The thought arose within her like an inner voice, "I love you, I always have and I always will. I really care for you and love you." She turned around, knelt at the chair, and putting her head in her hands began to sob. "O God, fill my emptiness. Please love me the way I've always wanted to be loved." That was a beginning. Within a month she underwent a dramatic conversion. She told me, "I experi-enced a flooding, a sense of God's complete forgiveness. And most of all, what I'd really wanted all my life—a clean heart." Reborn and restored, she got help, returned home, and was reconciled to her mother. Eventually she became the instrument through whom God reached several family members.

We have traced grace in some of its most important forms. In and through them all we cannot help but be struck by the Divine initiative. God is always first on the scene. Long before even "the creation of the world" (Ephesians 1:4) His grace had us in mind. And although Calvary occurred at a definite time and place within history, Jesus was "the Lamb that was slain from the creation of the world" (Revelation 13:8). Believe me, we have been recipients of grace (humanly speaking) for a long, long time. The way of grace is not some afterthought on God's part. It's *the* way, the *only* way God ever planned.

Ultimate Grace

This same grace will ultimately be our only basis for eternal fellowship with God in the life to come. In the final verse of the final chapter of the final book of Scripture, Revelation 22:21, John prays, "The grace of the Lord Jesus be with God's people. Amen." We can be sure every one of God's people who will worship and serve Him throughout eternity will be there for only *one reason— because they were recipients of grace—God's love freely given to the undeserving and the unworthy.* There is no other basis for entrance into the kingdom of God—here on earth or in heaven.

As a teenager, I attended many summer services held in the great holiness camp meetings of the Midwest. Sitting on the uncomfortable wooden benches, my feet touching the sawdust on the floor of the tabernacle, I listened in awe to some of the great evangelists of that day. I will always be grateful for their grace-filled messages. I remember often hearing descriptions of how it was going to be when we entered the gates of heaven. Inscribed over the arch of the entranceway, we were told, would be these words, "Whosoever will may come." But after we had entered in, if we were to look back at the gateway, we would see the words, "For by grace are you saved."

The House of the Hapsburgs had ruled the Austro-Hungarian Empire since 1273 and the family had been a major political power in Europe until the Great War of 1914-1918. The funeral of the Emperor Franz-Josef I of Austria was in November 1916.[4] It was the last of the grandiose imperial funerals to be staged.

The Hapsburgs are buried in the family crypt located in the basement of the Capucin Monastery of Vienna. On the day of the funeral, the entire court assembled in full white dress, their hats covered with ostrich plumes. A military band played somber dirges and an anthem by Haydn. The cortege wound its way down stairs illumined with flaming torches, bearing the coffin draped in the imperial colors, black and gold. Finally it reached the great iron doors of the crypt, behind which stood the Cardinal-Archbishop of Vienna, along with his entourage of high church officials.

The officer in charge of the procession was the Court Marshall. As he approached the closed door and pounded on it with the hilt of his ceremonial sword, he was following a ceremony prescribed from time immemorial. "Open!" he commanded.

"Who goes there?" intoned the Cardinal.

"We bear the remains of His Imperial and Apostolic Majesty, Franz-Josef I, by the Grace of God Emperor of Austria, King of Hungary, Defender of the Faith, Prince of Bohemia-Moravia, Grand Duke of Lombardy, Venezia, Styrgia. . . ." And so on, through the *thirty-seven titles* of the Emperor.

"We know him not," replied the Cardinal, from beyond the door. "Who goes there?"

"We bear the remains of His Majesty, Franz-Josef I, Emperor of Austria and King of Hungary"—this very abbreviated form was allowed only in dire emergencies.

"We know him not," came the Cardinal's reply again. "Who goes there?"

"We bear the body of Franz-Josef, *our brother, a sinner like us all!*"

Whereupon, the massive doors swung slowly open and Franz-Josef was borne within.

For it is by grace you have been saved,
through faith,
and this not from yourselves,
it is the gift of God.

Notes.

Chapter 1

1. See my book, *Healing for Damaged Emotions*, Wheaton, Illinois: Victor Books, 1981, pp. 79-84.
2. David Stoop, *Living With a Perfectionist*, Nashville: Oliver Nelson Books, 1987, p. 13.
3. *The American Heritage Dictionary of the English Language*, Wm. Morris, Editor, New York: Houghton Mifflin Co., 1973, p. 962.

Chapter 2

1. See my book, *Healing of Memories*, Wheaton, Illinois: Victor Books, 1985, pp. 95-122.
2. Unpublished scholarly paper, *Eyes That Cannot See: American Worldview and the Distortion of Grace*, Ralph Satter, 1987.

Chapter 3

1. *The American Heritage Dictionary of the English Language*, Wm. Morris, Editor, New York: Houghton Mifflin Co., 1973, p. 407; and Appendix, p. 1514.
2. Corrie ten Boom, *In My Father's House*, Old Tappan, New Jersey: Fleming H. Revell, 1976, p. 58.
3. Ken Magid and Carole McKelvey, *High Risk Children: Children Without Conscience*, Golden, Colorado: M and M Publishers, 1987.
4. *Ibid.*, p. 26.
5. Early Jabay, *The God Players* and *The Kingdom of the Self*, Grand Rapids: Zondervan Publishing House, 1969.

Chapter 4

1. Augustine, *The City of God*, Marcus Dods, Tr., in *Nicene and Post-Nicene Fathers*, book 14, vol. 2, Grand Rapids: William B. Eerdmans Publishing Company, 1983, p. 273.

Chapter 5

1. *The Encyclopedia Americana*, 1968 Edition, vol. 4, p. 532.

Chapter 6

1. Especially the writings of Karen Horney. Her books, *The Neurotic Personality of Our Time*, and *Neurosis and Human Growth*, New York: W.W. Norton Co., are classics in this field.
2. Horney, *Neurosis and Human Growth*, pp. 17-39.
3. *Ibid.*, pp. 187-290.

Chapter 7

1. A.W. Tozer, *The Knowledge of the Holy*, New York: Harper and Brothers Publishers, 1961, p. 100.
2. For a thorough discussion see William T. Kirwan, *Biblical Concepts for Christian Counseling*, Grand Rapids: Baker Book House, 1984, pp. 46-53.
3. *Ibid.*, p. 47. (Taken from Eerdman's *New Bible Dictionary*, p. 140).
4. *Ibid.*, pp. 47-51.

Chapter 9

1. For a detailed description of this form of inner healing and spiritual therapy, see my book, *Healing of Memories*, Wheaton, Illinois: Victor Books, 1985.

Chapter 10

1. See my book, *Healing for Damaged Emotions*, Wheaton, Illinois: Victor Books, 1981, p. 73.

Chapter 11

1. Charles Dickens, *Great Expectations* (Second Edition), New York: Holt and Rhinehart, 1972, p. 59.

Chapter 12

1. *The Institutes II*, ii, 15. Translated by John Allen. 2 Vols. Philadelphia Presbyterian Board of Publications, 1909, and *Commentary on Titus*, 1:12; cf. *Commentary on John*, 4:36. (Commentary on the Catholic Epistles. Translated by John Owen, Grand Rapids: William B. Eerdmans Publishing Company, 1948).
2. E. Stanley Jones, *The Way*, Nashville: Abingdon Press, 1946, pp. 19-60.
3. *Ibid.*, p. 43.
4. *The United Methodist Book of Hymns*, 1964, p. 98.
5. The details of this story were given to me by Dr. Ed McKinley, Professor of History, Asbury College.

11-23-94
P say